AGRICULTURAL LAND USE

I0408325

38 percent of the earth's surface is land

29.1 percent of the land is used for agriculture

Land Distribution
Percent

Permanent crops,[a] 4

Pastures, 68

Arable land, 28

Cropland Dedication
Percent

Other, 15

Sugar, 2

Roots and tubers, 3

Vegetables, 4

Fruits, 4

Pulses, 5

Oilseeds, 19

Grains, 48

Crop Use
Percent

Seed, 2

Industrial, 8

Feed, 14

Food, 43

Waste/ Loss,[b] 33

Irrigated vs. Nonirrigated Production
Percent

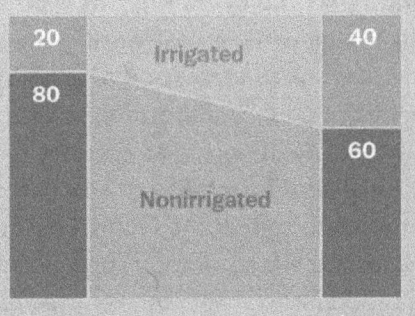

| 20 | Irrigated | 40 |
| 80 | Nonirrigated | 60 |

Field Distribution

Crops Produced

[a]Permanent crops refer to crops that last many years once planted, such as orchards, coffee, tea, nut trees, etc.
[b]Waste/Loss refers to the amount of crop production that is lost during growing, harvest, processing, distribution, and thrown out in the market or in the home.

Global Food Security

Key Judgments

Bottom Line: We judge that the overall risk of food insecurity[a] in many countries of strategic importance to the United States will increase during the next 10 years because of production, transport, and market disruptions to local food availability, lower purchasing power, and counterproductive government policies. Demographic shifts and constraints on key inputs, such as land and water, will probably compound the risk. In some countries, declining food security will almost certainly contribute to social disruptions and political instability. Simply growing more food globally will not lead to more food-secure countries because sustainable access will remain unequal; millions lack access to land or income sources to buy sufficient food. We judge that augmenting traditional approaches to agricultural development with lesser-used strategies—such as reducing crop and food waste, generating off-farm income activities, conducting research in minor crops[b], and fostering technical education in agriculture—would improve the resilience of local and global food systems. Such strategies can help Washington and its allies to develop creative complements to standard approaches and help resolve inherent tensions between goals such as producing more food and conserving water and other natural resources.

Increasing Food Insecurity

A. We judge that the overall risk of food insecurity in many countries of strategic importance to the United States will increase during the next 10 years because of production, transport, and market disruptions to local food availability, declining purchasing power, and counterproductive government policies. Demographic shifts and constraints on key inputs will compound this risk. In some countries, declining food security will almost certainly contribute to social disruptions or large-scale political instability or conflict, amplifying global concerns about the availability of food. We have moderate confidence in this judgment because we have a reliable and large body of reporting that correlates the effects of food supply disruptions, lower purchasing power, and poor policy choices with higher food insecurity. However, we are unable to pinpoint the thresholds and government actions that would result in these outcomes.

---

[a] The Intelligence Community defines *food security* as perceived and physical access to food supplies sufficient to meet basic needs and preferences at every level—individual, community, state, and global.
[b] The term *minor crops* refers to crops not generally sold on the global food market and consumed locally.

- Worsening food insecurity highlights the inadequacy of government institutions and developmental assistance to improve the resiliency of the agricultural sector and create sustainable safety-net programs for at-risk populations. Complicating these efforts, some governments and nongovernmental actors use food security as a political tool and do not seek increased food security for portions or all of their populations. Greater urbanization, population growth, and shifts toward a more protein-rich diet will intensify pressure on national and global markets.

- Threats to food availability during the next 10 years include climate change, extreme weather, conflict, diseases, resource constraints, and environmental degradation. For example, large exportable supplies of key components of food production—such as phosphates, potash, and fuel oil—come from states where conflict or government actions could cause supply chain disruptions that lead to price spikes.[c] In addition, monitoring and controlling outbreaks of agricultural diseases will become increasingly difficult as the world becomes more integrated, disease vectors shift, and domestic animal populations grow and become more concentrated.

- Many people will experience declining purchasing power—higher cost of food compared to wages—resulting from a wide array of factors. These include the loss of livelihoods, lack of employment opportunities, and higher food prices locally caused by increasing conflict, rapid population growth, and dwindling natural resource bases. Urban residents in most cases will be the first affected; however, a large percentage of rural residents in developing countries, who must also buy food, will see their purchasing power decline.

- The two food price spikes in 2007-2008 and 2010-2011 have increased the fervor with which some governments have implemented short-term food and agricultural policies that are likely to have adverse long-term effects. Governments attempting to secure political favor from certain groups or reduce their dependence on the world market for food have created trade restrictions, unattainable and inefficient self-sufficiency goals, and unsustainable social programs and agrarian reforms.

Regions at Risk

B. Prospects are poor for countries grappling with food insecurity. The majority of countries already experiencing high-to-extreme food insecurity[d] face risk factors that could worsen their food security through 2025; some countries that have low-to-moderate food insecurity today are at risk of experiencing worsening conditions during the next 10 years. The intersection of food insecurity with governance gaps will probably result in social disruption, political turmoil, or conflict. We have only moderate confidence in these judgments because we were not able to include all well-documented drivers of food insecurity in the methodology used for this assessment.

---

[c] See Annex C for a discussion of food supply and demand to include key agricultural commodities.
[d] See Annex B for a discussion of the methodology used to evaluate food insecurity.

- The increase in food insecurity is likely to be most prominent in Africa, the Middle East, and South Asia. The increase in risk factors will worsen already high levels of food insecurity in some countries and threaten to undermine governments that do not have sustainable food security policies.

- Most countries with increasing risk of worsening food insecurity are highly vulnerable to production disruptions resulting from environmental degradation, conflict, and disease. Such disruptions pose the greatest threat to food security in Africa and Asia, where subsistence and small-scale farmers and herders comprise the majority of the world's food-insecure population. Disruptions to production and transport corridors in major food-exporting countries will threaten national and global markets, creating fiscal strains for many countries reliant on food imports.

- Countries with rising exposure to food insecurity from lower purchasing power and counterproductive government policies are more prevalent in Africa, Asia, and Latin America. In many of these countries, government leases of state-owned land to domestic and foreign agricultural developers will stoke conflict in areas without well-defined land ownership laws and regulations.

Improving Food Access

C. We judge that augmenting traditional approaches to agricultural development with innovative, but lesser-used strategies—such as reducing crop and food waste, generating off-farm income activities, conducting research into minor crops,[e] and fostering technical education in agriculture— will improve the resilience of local and global food systems. This combination will probably increase the ability of individuals to acquire food and reinforce US developmental strategies more than either approach alone. We have high confidence in these judgments because we have reliable open source information and academic research on the value of both traditional and nontraditional approaches to improve the resilience of local and global food systems.

Simply growing more food will not result in more food-secure countries. As a whole, the world is likely to continue to produce sufficient food supplies for at least the next 10 years, but food distribution will almost certainly remain uneven because tens of millions of people lack access to arable land or income sources to buy food.

- Because approximately one-third of the food produced globally does not get consumed due to losses and waste—and the amount of arable land and water available for food production is limited—the greatest potential to relieve food scarcity will be through investments in infrastructure, technology, and education to improve the food supply chain while using fewer resources. Less than 5 percent of all agricultural research and development (R&D) is expended on reducing food losses and waste, according to academic research.

- The creation of rural nonfarm-wage jobs, such as agroprocessing and construction, would establish a buffer and coping mechanism for families in times when harvests might suffer from unfavorable

---

[e] The term *minor crops* refers to crops not generally sold on the global food market and consumed locally.

Use of Sensor To Adjust Fertilizer Application

This high-clearance sprayer makes variable-rate nitrogen applications to corn based on sensor readings. The sensors—the white camera-like modules on the outriggers—monitor plant stresses that are frequently related to nitrogen status.

Use of Global Positioning System (GPS)

In Missouri, an agricultural engineer examines corn from this combine's grain flow sensor. The combine is linked to the satellite-based GPS, allowing precise yield and location data to be correlated with soil samples taken earlier throughout the field. This information will help growers plan best fertilizer rates for the next crop.

GPS antenna

Source: USDA Agriculture Research Service (ARS).

weather or other disruptions. This source of income might also reduce rapid urbanization as well as natural resource degradation resulting from overexploitation. Income from these jobs would probably spur investment in the agricultural sector; farming families could use some of this income to improve their land or purchase farming tools.

- We assess that increased funding for agricultural education in both developing and developed countries would help provide the skilled labor force needed to meet the demands of a changing food system. Most developing countries face a critical shortage of the skilled labor needed to improve the global and local agricultural chains. In developed countries, more positions are created in agriculture each year than there are domestic college graduates with agricultural degrees to fill them.

- Traditional agricultural assistance to complement the lesser-used strategies includes developing and deploying new and existing agricultural technologies, improving water, soil, and land management, expanding and modernizing trade infrastructure, and enhancing agricultural policies and institutional capacities.

Implications for the United States

D. Developing creative complements to traditional approaches to improve global food security will take a worldwide effort. Opportunities exist for the United States—already viewed as a leader in promoting global food security—to align with long-standing allies as well as new partners. Some countries offer nontraditional models of how to resolve the inherent tension between goals such as producing more food and conserving water and other natural resources. Emerging economies with growing food security expertise can offer solutions more palatable to countries with low levels of development and technology. Food-insecure countries themselves will also be an important part of the effort; those taking complete or partial ownership of programs designed to build local food security are likely to see more sustainable results.

- Because the United States is a major source of agricultural technology and innovation, many countries will expect it to continue to develop and share advanced food technologies. More poor countries, however, are seeking south-south cooperation on agricultural technology issues because of regional dietary preferences and expertise in small-scale water, land, and crop management practices. This positions some countries to gain greater global influence through their agricultural research programs.

- Developing countries will expect the United States to adapt its agricultural development operations to better suit these countries' limited abilities to use first-world technologies, especially in areas that lack reliable electricity and maintenance capacity for agriculture infrastructure.

- Many countries would probably welcome assistance to increase the institutional capacity of their governments to address domestic food-security concerns. Efforts designed to change subsistence farms into small-and mid-sized commercial enterprises are more likely to be effective at increasing sustainable food security than rapidly promoting large-scale, industrial agriculture operations.

This page has been intentionally left blank.

Contents

Discussion

Annexes

Scope Note

22 September 2015

Scope
This Assessment was prepared under the auspices of the Director, Strategic Futures Group (SFG) and drafted by the Central Intelligence Agency. It was coordinated with DIA, NGA, NSA, DOE, DHS, State/INR, and the ODNI. Information available as of April 2015 was used in the preparation of this product.

The time frame for the Key Judgments is out to 2025; however, we also discuss longer-term trends that might affect US national security interests.

For this Assessment, we conducted detailed unclassified research (see Annex A) on food security issues in multiple countries and across six food-related commodities (see Annex C). The six principal food commodities analyzed compose an average of 76 percent of calories and 46 percent of proteins consumed globally.

Assumptions
We assume that the principal demand factors that will affect food security in the long term (beyond 2025) are demographic changes (to include urbanization) and income growth in emerging and developing countries. These trends will influence dietary preferences. The principal supply factors will be: weather (extreme events and climate change), the rate of agricultural technology development and deployment, the availability of resources (land, fertilizer, water, capital, etc.), and government policies (including investment choices, export controls, biofuel mandates, and land and water management). We assume that agricultural markets, energy availability, agricultural technologies, and supporting infrastructure will not lead to dramatic, "discontinuous" changes in food supply or demand by 2025.

Estimative Language
Estimates of likelihood convey judgments about the probability of developments or events. Confidence levels provide assessments on the quality and quantity of source information. Annex G (Estimative Language) elaborates on these terms.

Definitions

The Intelligence Community defines *food security* as perceived and actual physical access to food supplies sufficient to meet basic needs and preferences at every level—individual, community, state, and global.

The US Department of Agriculture's (USDA's) definition of food security includes at a minimum:

- The ready availability of nutritionally adequate and safe foods, and

- An assured ability to acquire acceptable foods in socially acceptable ways (without resorting to emergency food supplies, scavenging, stealing, or other coping strategies).

USAID defined food security in 1992 as "when all people at all times have both physical and economic access to sufficient food to meet their dietary needs for a productive and healthy life."

The United Nations World Food Summit of 1996 defined food security as existing "when all people at all times have access to sufficient, safe, nutritious food to maintain a healthy and active life." Food security is also defined as including both physical and economic access to food that meets people's dietary needs as well as their food preferences.

Most experts agree that food security is composed of the following dimensions:

- Food availability – sufficient quantities of food are available on a consistent basis.

- Food access – sufficient resources are available to obtain appropriate foods for a nutritious diet.

- Food use – food is able to be utilized appropriately based on knowledge of basic nutrition and care, as well as adequate water and sanitation for nutrient absorption.

We use the following degrees to assess food insecurity:

- **Extreme food insecurity** – Widespread malnutrition exists, causing possible localized deaths due to starvation or malnutrition-related diseases.

- **High food insecurity** – The population's diet is calorie-deficient and unbalanced with localized high malnutrition rates.

- **Moderate food insecurity** – The population's caloric intake is mostly sufficient, but its diet is unbalanced.

- **Low food insecurity** – The population's diet generally meets most caloric and nutrient needs.

Food losses refer to the decrease in edible food mass throughout the part of the supply chain that specifically leads to edible food for human consumption. Food losses occurring at the end of the food chain, which are caused by retailers' and consumers' behavior, are called *food waste*.

Undernutrition is defined by UNICEF as the outcome of insufficient food intake and repeated infectious diseases. It includes being underweight for one's age, too short for one's age (stunted), dangerously thin for one's height (wasted), and deficient in vitamins and minerals (micronutrient malnutrition).

Production Projections

The UN Food and Agriculture Organization estimates the world will need to produce 60 percent more food by 2050. Growth in consumption for animal products will increase the demand for animal feeds, such as corn and soybeans. Meeting this demand most likely will require efforts beyond simply expanding acreage and increasing crop and livestock productivity because of the potential negative consequences of land use change to livelihoods and the environment.

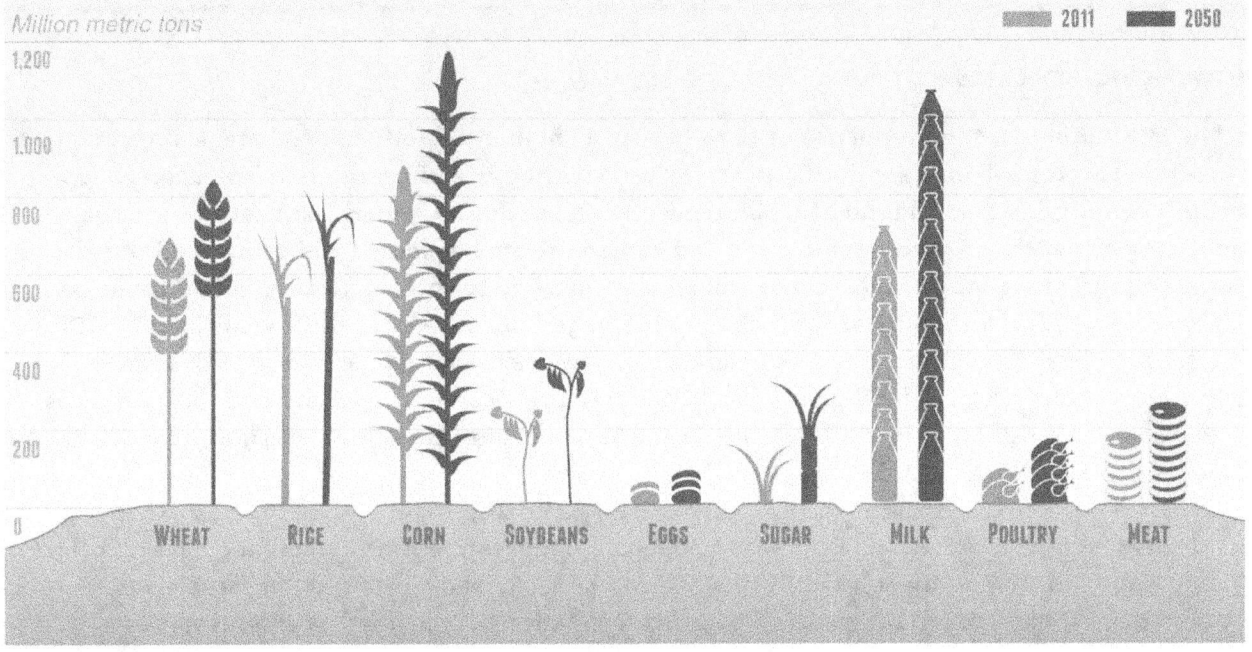

Million metric tons

2011   2050

1,200

1,000

800

600

400

200

0

WHEAT   RICE   CORN   SOYBEANS   EGGS   SUGAR   MILK   POULTRY   MEAT

Global Food Security

Discussion

Increasing Food Insecurity

KJ A. We judge that the overall risk of food insecurity in many countries of strategic importance to the United States will increase during the next 10 years because of production, transport, and market disruptions to local food availability, declining purchasing power, and counterproductive government policies. Demographic shifts and constraints on key inputs will compound this risk. In some countries, declining food security will almost certainly contribute to social disruptions or large-scale political instability or conflict, amplifying global concerns about the availability of food. We have moderate confidence in this judgment because we have a reliable and large body of reporting that correlates the effects of food supply disruptions, lower purchasing power, and poor policy choices with higher food insecurity. However, we are unable to pinpoint the thresholds and government actions that would result in these outcomes.

- Increasing food insecurity highlights the inadequacy of government institutions and developmental assistance to improve the resiliency of the agricultural sector and create sustainable safety-net programs for at-risk populations. Complicating these efforts, some governments, as well as nongovernmental actors, use food security as a political tool and do not seek increased food security for a portion or all of their populations. Greater urbanization, population growth, and shifts toward a more protein-rich diet also will intensify pressure on national and global markets.

Threats to Local Food Availability

We assess that a heightened risk of climate change effects, extreme weather events, conflict, disease spread, and environmental degradation are likely to cause disruptions to local, regional, and global food supplies during the next 10 years. In some cases, these dynamics will interact. For example, warmer temperatures might lead to disease spread or prolonged drought, prompting rapid rural migration to cities. In turn, urban slums may become hotbeds for unrest.

Weather and Climate Pressures. We judge that weather and climate patterns to 2025 will be key in determining local and regional crop production and will be a dominant factor contributing to the volatility of food prices. Extreme weather events, including droughts, floods, and extended periods of extreme temperatures, as well as catastrophic events such as tropical cyclones, will threaten agricultural production. Africa and Asia will be the regions where food security is most affected. Long-term climate

1

trends and natural resource constraints (for example, land, water, and energy) will also put upward pressure on food prices[f].

- We judge there is a high risk that at least one region-wide drought will occur in the Horn of Africa and the Sahel regions during the next 10 years. Such a drought could stoke conflict and require large amounts of international food assistance to prevent famine.

Conflict. We judge that existing and new episodes of large-scale domestic political instability or internal conflict will continue to threaten access to food because such turmoil threatens livelihoods and local food availability and degrades resources. In the short term, instability interrupts food-distribution systems, farming, and other employment activities and degrades basic services. Food prices also often rise because of the declining availability of food and the prevalence of hoarding. Over the long term, the loss of assets, such as farming equipment, and the destruction of land and water resources and infrastructure—combined with the potential loss of skilled labor—will impede the recovery of most countries after a conflict has subsided.

- In 2004, during Western Sudan's Darfur conflict, tactics such as cutting down fruit trees and destroying irrigation ditches were used to eradicate farmers' claims to land and ruin livelihoods, according to academic research. The United Nations Children's Fund (UNICEF) estimated that 4.7 million people experienced reduced food security because of the conflict.

- A UN Food and Agriculture Organization (FAO) analysis concluded that global agricultural losses due to conflict between 1970 and 1997 averaged $4.3 billion annually (in 1995 constant US dollars), exceeding the value of food aid to the affected countries. For example, the 1977-1992 Mozambique civil war and the 1994 Rwandan genocide reduced both countries' national cattle herds—the primary asset for most pastoralists—by 80 and 50 percent, respectively, according to academic reporting.

Disease. We judge that monitoring and controlling agricultural and human disease outbreaks that affect food security will become increasingly difficult as the world becomes more integrated and domestic animal populations expand and become more concentrated. Diseases that can be transmitted from animals to humans and vice versa, such as the ebolavirus and avian flu, will continue to disrupt farming and marketing activities, causing price spikes and impeding economic growth.

- Increased globalized trade in agricultural goods—although it will improve food availability in many food-deficit nations—will almost certainly accelerate the spread of plant and livestock diseases. Outbreaks of such diseases will probably increase as the pace of trade quickens. The USDA projects during the next 10 years, that global grain trade will increase by 25, 35, 19, and 36 percent, respectively, for coarse grains, rice, wheat, and soybeans—which comprise 75 percent of the caloric base of the world's population. These production-growth percentages all exceed expected global population growth during this time frame. Global trade in meat and poultry also is projected to increase 22 percent during the same period.

---

[f] See Annex D for a discussion of the food, water, and energy nexus.

- The global die-off of pollinators, such as bees, caused by chemicals, diseases, pests, and poor nutrition already is causing extensive agricultural losses, especially of fruits and vegetables. Increasing temperatures due to climate change also are introducing pests to new regions. Such pests could harm local food security by spreading plant diseases, such as the spread of coffee rust in Central America and East Africa, where millions depend on the crop for their livelihoods, according to press reporting.

- Deforestation is likely to increase the interaction of wildlife and livestock. The UN estimates that up to 270 million hectares of additional forests—about the size of Colorado—could be converted to pastureland by 2030. Such measures increase the threat of new outbreaks of livestock diseases. Aquaculture also is likely to be a source of increasing disease outbreaks in future years, given the speed of the industry's growth, weak regulation, and the heavy concentration of fish stocks.

Environmental Degradation. We judge that depleted and degraded groundwater and soils—including reduced soil moisture storage capacity and fertility—will lead to local production disruptions that will reduce food security. Land degradation, drought, desertification, and loss in fertile soil cost up to 5 percent of world agricultural gross domestic production—or about $450 billion—annually, according to a study presented at the UN Convention to Combat Desertification. Many of the world's most food-insecure people live in rural areas that suffer from deforestation, salinization, soil erosion, desertification, and degraded pastures and water sources.

- About 25 percent of arable soil worldwide is highly degraded and often requires large supplies of fertilizers and other inputs to remain productive. This is most pronounced in highly populated areas, including China, India, Pakistan, and the Great Lakes and Sahel regions of Africa, according to the UN. Poor land-management practices, including overgrazing, the expansion of unsuitable cash-crop cultivation, single cropping, and improper application of modern methods, can decrease the fertility of soils and encourage erosion, leading to increased land degradation that contributes to a decrease in crop yields.

- Large irrigation schemes around the world have created soil and water salinity problems and in many countries in Central Asia, where more than 16 million hectares of irrigated land are salinized, according to the FAO. Globally, the FAO estimates that 45 million hectares, or 19.5 percent of irrigated land, is salt-affected compared to 32 million hectares, or only 2 percent of land devoted to rain-fed agriculture.

Declining Purchasing Power

We assess that many countries will experience declining purchasing power—higher cost of food compared to wages—because of the loss of livelihoods, lack of employment opportunities, and higher food prices. Underlying causes include increasing conflict, rapid population growth, and dwindling natural resource bases. Urban residents in most cases will be the first affected; however, a large percentage of rural residents in developing countries also need to buy food and will see their purchasing power decline.

- The number of people living in extreme poverty—earning only $1.25 per day—has decreased significantly during the past three decades, according to the World Bank, although East Asia accounts for the majority of this decrease. Sub-Saharan Africa and South Asia—regions that will face some of the greatest challenges to improving food security—now account for 80 percent of the world's extreme poor. Many countries are likely to see continued declining wages compared to the cost of food, according to diplomatic and open source reporting.

- We assess that trends in conflict and extreme weather will increase the risk that households will have their livelihoods disrupted. Forced displacement is at the highest level in the post-World War II era—accounting for more than 59 million people as of June 2015, according to UN—and we assess that this trend is not likely to abate. Conflicts in Africa and the Middle East continue to drive people from their homes and livelihoods, according to the UN High Commissioner for Refugees. Extreme weather events, such as droughts and storms, are likely to negatively affect a larger number of people during the next 10 years as population growth, among other factors, in many countries forces more people to reside in areas most prone to disasters.

- If current trends continue, global unemployment will increase during the next several years—especially for young adults—reaching more than 215 million jobseekers by 2018, compared to 202 million in 2013, according to the International Labor Organization. During this period, around 40 million net new jobs will be created every year—fewer than the 42.6 million people that are expected to enter the labor market annually. The youth-to-adult unemployment ratio, which has reached a historical peak, is particularly high in the Middle East and North Africa, as well as in parts of Latin America, the Caribbean, and Southern Europe.

Counterproductive Government Policies

In response to the two food price spikes during the past decade (in 2008 and 2011), governments implemented short-term food and agricultural policies that will probably have adverse long-term effects. Governments attempting to secure political favor from certain groups or reduce their dependence on the world market for food have created trade restrictions, inefficient self-sufficiency goals, and unsustainable social programs and agrarian reforms.

- Between 2007 and 2011, more than 30 major food exporters restricted trade in order to stem rising domestic food inflation; this move caused global food prices to surge. The international price of rice tripled in early 2008 a few months after several major exporters restricted rice exports. Russia's decision to ban their grain exports in July 2010 increased global prices by about 46 percent the following month.

- Many countries with dwindling water resources have sought to expand their domestic production through water-intensive measures. Insufficient water availability, negative environmental effects, and poor economic viability are likely to hamper many projects.

Shifting Demographics

We assess that demographic shifts will increase the risk of food insecurity. World population is projected to grow by about 900 million between 2014 and 2025; rapidly expanding urban centers will experience the highest growth in food demand.

Population Growth and Urbanization. Some 95 percent of the world's population growth will occur in developing nations during the next 20 years. The rate of growth will be the fastest in countries that are the most food insecure and have the least capacity to adapt. Urbanization will undermine food security in a number of ways, including the loss of prime arable land to residential construction, competition for water resources, more food losses through increased use of inefficient transportation networks, and a need for more wage-paying employment and safety-net programs.

- Fertility rates have not fallen as expected in many parts of Sub-Saharan Africa; thus the pace of development in some of the world's least developed countries will probably slow. According to the UN Population Division's (UNPD's) updated projections, the population of Sub-Saharan Africa will reach about 2.15 billion in 2050, up from a previously projected 1.96 billion.

- In many African and Asian countries, the average farm size is falling steadily as land continues to be subdivided, often through cultural inheritance customs. This leads to migration to urban areas because these smaller plots of land are insufficient to provide livelihoods unless other forms of rural income are available.

- The FAO estimates that the world must increase food production by 50 to 60 percent to satisfy global population growth and changing consumption patterns by 2050. Food consumption per capita in advanced economies has mostly peaked, but the predicted annual real GDP per capita growth rate is 5.1 percent for emerging and developing economies between now and 2020, according to the IMF. This growth will almost certainly prompt increased consumption of meat, dairy, and processed foods per capita.

Constraints on Key Inputs

Agriculture will increasingly compete with other economic sectors for critical inputs (water, land, and energy) as countries become more urbanized and development projects focus on expanding industries and services. As cities grow, they will occupy some of the most fertile agricultural land with the easiest access to markets; industries will demand more water and energy. Tradeoffs—such as natural gas for fertilizer production or heating—will occur more frequently.

Water. Between now and 2025, global demand for fresh water will increase, but the supply will not keep pace with demand without more effective management of water resources. More than a billion people currently live in water-scarce regions; as many as 3.5 billion could experience water scarcity by 2025, according to the World Bank. Agriculture consumes 70 percent of the global freshwater supply, and 40 percent of the world's agriculture depends on irrigation.

- To satisfy growing food demand, several countries in Asia, North America, Africa, and nearly all countries in the Middle East and North Africa have over pumped their groundwater—extracting more of this resource than is replenished—according to academic research. As a result, their agricultural production will probably be constrained by a decline in either the quality or quantity of water available to them during the next 10 years.

- Over the long term, without mitigating actions, the exhaustion of groundwater sources will cause some countries' food production to decline, and their food demand will have to be increasingly satisfied through global markets.

TOP IRRIGATORS

Country	Area Equipped for Irrigation[a] (million hectares)	Share of Cropland Irrigated (percent)
India	66.7	39
China	64.5	52
US	23.0	14
Pakistan	20.2	95
Iran	9.1	48
Indonesia	6.7	16
Thailand	6.4	34
Mexico	6.3	23
Turkey	5.2	21
Bangladesh	5.1	60
Vietnam	4.6	48
Brazil	4.5	7
Russia	4.3	3
Uzbekistan	4.2	91
Italy	3.9	42
Other	76.8	NA
World total	**311.7**	**20**

[a]Not all area equipped for irrigation will be in use.
Note: Due to rounding, total figures may not match.
Source: UN FAO, 2009.

Fertilizer and Fuel. Exportable supplies of several primary agricultural inputs, such as fertilizer ingredients, are in regions of the world that are vulnerable to political and economic stresses. The price of fuel, in part determined by turmoil in oil-producing countries and global economic conditions, will also be a factor in food availability because of the use of fuel in most segments of the supply chain, from running irrigation pumps to transporting food to markets.

- Large, high-quality deposits of rock phosphate, a major fertilizer ingredient, are concentrated in North Africa, the Middle East, Asia, and North America. Morocco and China control about 80 percent of known reserves globally, according to USGS. Additional reserves are located in unstable countries or regions. In 2013, seven countries accounted for 93 percent of global unprocessed phosphate exports, according to trade data.

- Potash—produced in only a few countries—is another critical fertilizer ingredient, especially for the production of corn and soybeans.

- Supplies of fuel and natural gas are likely to remain sufficient on the global market, but many low- and middle-income importing countries will probably be unable—at current and projected prices—to sustain subsidies that increase supplies to support agricultural production.

Land. During the next 10 years, the FAO estimates that only 20 percent of the increase in agricultural production, including more than 450 million additional tons of grain and oilseed production, will result from the expansion of cultivation into new land. All of the increase in the amount of land under cultivation will come from developing countries because land used for agriculture is declining in the developed world. Most of this expansion will occur in Latin America and Sub-Saharan Africa. Cultivation of some of this land remains difficult because of the higher input costs per hectare, which make such cultivation uneconomical under current market conditions. In addition, much of this land is either environmentally unsound or currently is pastureland.

Regions at Risk

KJ B. Prospects are poor for countries grappling with food insecurity. The majority of countries already experiencing high-to-extreme food insecurity[9] face risk factors that could worsen their food security through 2025. Some countries that have low-to-moderate food insecurity today are at risk of experiencing worsening conditions during the next 10 years. The intersection of food insecurity with governance gaps will probably result in social disruption, political turmoil, or conflict. We have only moderate confidence in these judgments because we were not able to include all well-documented drivers of food insecurity in the methodology used to produce this assessment.

- Risk factors will worsen already high levels of food insecurity in several countries, and threaten to undermine governments that lack sustainable food security policies, and exacerbate the depletion of natural resources in others.

- Most countries with increasing risk of rising food insecurity have high vulnerabilities to production disruptions from environmental degradation, conflict, and disease. Such disruptions will be the greatest threat to food security in Africa and Asia, where subsistence and small-scale farmers and herders comprise the majority of the world's food insecure. Disruptions to production and transport corridors in major food-exporting countries will threaten national and global markets, creating financial strains for many countries reliant on food imports.

- Countries with rising exposure to food insecurity due to lower purchasing power and counterproductive government policies are more prevalent in Africa, Asia, and Latin America. In many of these countries, government leases of state-owned land to domestic and foreign agricultural developers will stoke conflict in areas without well-defined land ownership laws and regulations. In addition, clashes between farmers and pastoralists will probably increase as these two groups compete for the same resources. (See textbox on page 9 for an expanded discussion of conflict resulting from food insecurity.)

Outlook by Region

Africa. Most countries in **Sub-Saharan Africa** are at risk of worsening food insecurity, largely because of political instability or low-level conflict, population growth, and environmental degradation. The risk of growing food insecurity for countries in **North Africa** is increasing because of population growth, high unemployment—especially among young adults—and economic and employment disruptions resulting from conflict.

- **The Horn of Africa and Sahel**, especially, present microcosms of high humanitarian, geopolitical, and security costs associated with chronic food insecurity. Recurring severe food shortages and competition for resources will continue to fuel instability at local, national, and subregional levels.

- Although the prevalence of undernutrition in Sub-Saharan Africa is declining, the number of undernourished people continues to climb along with increasing population, according to the FAO's State of Food Insecurity 2014 report. In North Africa, the prevalence of undernutrition and the

---

[9] See Annex B for a discussion of the methodology used to evaluate food insecurity.

number of undernourished people has doubled since 2010, primarily because of the conflicts in the region.

The Middle East. About half of the countries in the Middle East are at risk of worsening food security, and the prevalence of undernutrition in the Middle East continues to climb, according to the FAO. Conflict and reduced water availability are the risk factors most prominent in the region. We judge that escalating conflict and lower purchasing power will probably pose the greatest risks to food security for countries in the region that currently have a moderate-to-low food insecurity risk.

- The Middle East is the only region in the world that has experienced an increase in the percentage of food-insecure people since 1990, according to the FAO's State of Food Insecurity 2014 report. The number of undernourished people has increased by more than 10 million, and the percent of the population that is undernourished has grown by almost 40 percent.

Asia. Most countries in South Asia are at increasing risk of worsening food insecurity, although fewer countries in Southeast, East, and Central Asia face an increasing risk of worsening food security through 2025. The pressures from population growth, water stress, and environmental degradation create the greatest number of risk factors for increased food insecurity in the region. Several countries in the region have over pumped their ground water resources and will be at increased risk of food insecurity.

Latin America. With a few exceptions, Latin America overall has lower risks of increasing food insecurity than most other regions. Countries at risk face a combination of counterproductive government policies and extreme weather patterns that threaten their agriculture.

Small Island Developing States *(SIDS).* We assess that most SIDS, 51 states from the Pacific, Atlantic, and Indian Oceans and the Caribbean, Mediterranean, and South China Seas, already face worsening environmental conditions and few employment opportunities. The effects of climate change will almost certainly increase the risks for worsening food insecurity. Some Pacific island countries already have begun voluntary inter- and intra-state relocation in anticipation of sea level rise, increased storm surges, other coastal hazards, and environmental degradation such as salt water intrusion. All these factors threaten food security and livelihoods.

- Most SIDS have limited land area for agriculture and often rely on imports because of the low diversity of domestically produced crops and food products. Relative isolation and the long distances to major import and export markets also result in higher food prices and extreme susceptibility to external shocks.

- Declining fisheries production from a warming ocean would also have a particularly adverse effect on Pacific island countries, where fish are the main source of animal protein and tuna fishing, in particular, is a critical source of revenue and employment.

- General weakness in the public sector because of declining fiscal revenues is a further major challenge to agricultural and rural development in many SIDS. The agricultural sector faces a lack of competitiveness, an aging population, low levels of investment, and increased scarcity of natural resources, often worsened by natural disasters.

Lower-Level Conflict Most Likely Form of Instability

We assess that major food-related interstate conflict (war) is unlikely through 2025, but that lesser forms of conflict and tension—both between groups within countries and between countries—will increase for three reasons. First, small-scale clashes between farmers and pastoralists—including cross-border skirmishes—will rise as government policies, natural resource constraints, and pressure due to climate change push these two groups into closer proximity. Second, terrorists, militants, and international crime organizations will probably seek to increase their control over food sources to recruit members, boost earnings, and promote their own interests. Third, disputes over shared marine fisheries[h] and major river basins will probably rise as countries vie for control over increasingly scarce resources.

- We judge that government grants of state-owned land to domestic and foreign agricultural developers in Sub-Saharan Africa and Southeast Asia could prompt low-level conflict in areas without well-defined land ownership laws and regulations. In many of the countries targeted for large land leases, the government retains ownership and controls decisionmaking. In addition, many of these countries lack land tenure laws and protection for communal and grazing lands, according to the Brookings Institution.

- Insurgent groups are likely to take advantage of food insecurity in countries where the central government has little control over large swaths of territory. These groups will almost certainly capitalize on poor conditions, exploit international food aid, and discredit governments that are unable or unwilling to address the food needs of their populations. The success of drug cartels in extorting money from legitimate agricultural producers also might push other criminal elements to use similar methods; drug cartels have targeted agriculture when counterdrug operations have limited their drug revenue.

Disputes among countries are likely to increase as fishermen are forced to travel further from shore into contested waters due to the depletion of marine fisheries, especially in the South China Sea. We judge that such disputes might combine with other sources of friction to create a higher risk of conflict.

---

[h] See Annex F for a discussion of the South China Sea and Indian Ocean Fisheries.

Improving Food Access

KJ C. We judge that augmenting traditional approaches to agricultural development with innovative, but lesser-used strategies—such as reducing crop and food waste, generating off-farm income activities, conducting research into minor crops[i], and fostering technical education in agriculture—will improve the resilience of local and global food systems. This combination will probably increase the ability of individuals to acquire food and reinforce US developmental strategies more than either approach alone. We have high confidence in these judgments because we have reliable open source information and academic research on the value of both traditional and nontraditional approaches to improve the resilience of local and global food systems.

Simply growing more food will not result in more food-secure countries. As a whole, the world is likely to continue to produce sufficient food supplies for at least the next 10 years, but food distribution will almost certainly remain uneven because tens of millions of people lack access to arable land or income sources to buy food.

- Current development programs often fail to consider the recipient's capacity to use or maintain first-world technologies. For example, some high-yielding varieties of grain crops are more susceptible to loss unless paired with modern storage and processing techniques often unavailable to small-scale farmers in developing countries.

- For improvements in infrastructure systems to be effective over the long term, host governments and local communities must have the capacity to support maintenance and repair.

- Creating multiplier effects through complementary initiatives, including combining infectious disease-control efforts with food-security schemes, might increase food supplies and reduce the need for food aid in the long term. For example, the global initiative to eradicate river blindness[j] brought 25 million hectares of previously uninhabitable land into agricultural production. Combining programs that address improved sanitation infrastructure with increased food production would also improve overall food security because diseases and parasites from poor sanitation infrastructure inhibit the absorption of nutrients and calories.

Lesser-Used Strategies
Reducing Food Losses and Waste. Because approximately one-third of the food produced globally does not get consumed due to losses and waste—and the amount of arable land and water available for food production is limited—the greatest potential for relief from food scarcity will be through investments in infrastructure, technology, and education to improve the food supply chain while using fewer resources. Less than 5 percent of all agricultural research and development (R&D) is expended on reducing food losses and waste.

- Employing lessons learned from human infectious-disease control, including education, surveillance, and containment, would almost certainly help mitigate disease and contamination loss in livestock as well as grain crops. For example, 5 billion people annually are exposed to aflatoxins—carcinogenic

---

[i] The term *minor crops* refers to crops not generally sold on the global food market and consumed locally.
[j] River blindness is an eye and skin disease caused by a tiny worm called *Onchoncerca vulvulus* spread by bites of infected blackflies.

10

toxins produced by a soil-borne fungus that can develop in improperly stored crops. Such toxins lead to reduced supplies of grain and fodder and diminish the health of animals as well as humans.

- Using the power of the media to educate and encourage consumers to avoid food waste, similar to water conservation campaigns, would probably lead to significant reductions in the costs of subsidy programs and lost resources. For example, Turkey's campaign to reduce bread waste, launched in 2013, reduced daily bread losses by 18 percent and produced savings of $1.5 billion, according to an OECD-FAO report. Such campaigns could be especially effective in developed countries and those countries with food subsidies that provide for the whole population, not just those in need.

- Expanded application of existing irradiation technology could reduce food losses—which can be as high as 50 percent in developing countries—by reducing bacteria and fungus that quicken spoilage of food products. However, the technology has met with minor public resistance because the process can alter the flavor, texture, and nutritional composition of some foods.

Developing and deploying improved types of storage and transportation methods, especially those designed for use by smaller stakeholders and markets, would improve food security by reducing losses. Fruits, vegetables, and tree crops offer a way for farmers with smaller plots of land to increase their incomes and diversify their nutrition sources. Unless farmers have access to markets, transportation, and storage, however, the likelihood of increased waste is high.

- Assisting national and local governments in building and maintaining national and community reserve stocks in modern storage facilities, especially in countries with high temperatures and highly variable rainfall, would allow countries to buy and store greater amounts of excess food production during good harvest years. This would help governments mitigate short-term food insecurity through domestic interventions that would be less costly and more rapid than international aid deployment; this approach would also create an economic buffer for farmers.

- The increased use of container versus bulk shipping in certain markets would probably increase delivery options for shippers and end users, reduce cargo losses during shipment, and facilitate faster turnaround times. The regularity of container shipping services—ships typically call at each port in specific rotation weekly or biweekly—provides predictable scheduling for logistics planners. In addition, containerized cargo is less likely to suffer damage from the elements.

Generating Off-Farm Income. Creating rural nonfarm-wage jobs, such as those involved in the processing of farm products—sometimes called "agroprocesssing"—and construction, would build a buffer and coping mechanism for families during poor harvests. This source of income might also reduce rapid urbanization as well as natural resource degradation through overexploitation. Income from such jobs would also probably spur investment in the agricultural sector.

- Farmers with small plots of land—80 percent of the world's farmers work less than 2 acres of land—are unlikely to be able to rise above the poverty level by growing staple crops. Landless farm workers account for tens of millions of the world's most food-insecure people, and demand for farm labor is generally low during non-planting and non-harvest times.

- Rural nonfarm income could alleviate the lack of available credit by providing farmers with cash to invest in productivity-enhancing inputs. Furthermore, the development of wage jobs in the food system, such as distributing and selling farm inputs, could increase the profitability of farming through cheaper inputs and greater market access.

Conducting Research in Minor Crops. Public and private research and investment is very low for many root crops and locally adapted small grains, but these foods can help combat food shortages in drought-prone areas and are already familiar to local communities. More than 90 percent of global agricultural research—the majority funded by the private sector—currently is conducted in developed countries and is focused on crops important to those economies given these a higher rate of return on investment. In most developing countries, public funds—generally small amounts—are still the major source of support for agricultural research; the private sector accounts for just 6 percent.

- Additional research and infrastructure investment in cassava could boost global food supplies and farmer incomes because of its ability to grow well in harsh conditions, its multi-purpose uses—such as food, animal feed, and biofuel—and its wide familiarity among food-insecure populations in Sub-Saharan Africa, Latin America, and Asia. Research is needed to improve cassava's nutritional value—it has the lowest protein content of all staple food crops—and reduce its susceptibility to disease. Cassava could become a more important global biofuel feedstock and animal feed, especially for export to Asia, as traditional feed stocks, such as corn and sugar, remain in tight supply.

- In Africa, finger millet, teff, and fonio are nutritious, fast-growing small grains better suited for low-fertility, dry soil than Western crops such as wheat and corn. But yields are comparatively low for these crops because of the lack of investment in developing new varieties as well as suboptimal farming and processing techniques.

- Salt-tolerant plants that can produce fodder, food, and feedstock for biofuels might be suitable for use on approximately 130 million hectares of salt-contaminated land worldwide. Some salt-tolerant crops have biomass yields similar to alfalfa and oil yields comparable to soybeans. Integration of saline agriculture with aquaculture can produce both salt-tolerant crops and high-quality protein.

Fostering Technical Education in Agriculture. Increased funding for agricultural education opportunities targeted at both developing and developed countries would help provide the skilled labor force needed to meet the demands of a changing food system. Foundations and other donors are funding and facilitating access to advanced technologies on a wide range of crops, but technical advances have outpaced the availability of trained personnel, creating a large gap in the ability of governments and development organizations to integrate and use these technologies effectively.

- Most developing countries face a critical shortage of the skilled labor needed to improve the whole agricultural chain, including officials trained in outreach to small-scale farmers and herders. In developed countries, more positions are created in agriculture each year than there are domestic college graduates with agricultural degrees to fill them.

- In most developing countries, young people associate agriculture with a lifetime of poverty. Therefore, government employment schemes to keep young people in the rural sectors will probably have the best results if they frame agriculture as a business—providing ways to create value added—rather than focusing solely on increasing agricultural output.

- Teaching more advanced agricultural skills as part of military training—including programs tailored to retiring soldiers, counterinsurgency programs, or "Phase-Zero"[k] operations—would provide better opportunities to transition soldiers into the work force after their tours are complete.

- Countries with a shortage of skilled personnel might benefit from establishing regional research centers that create economies of scale to help attract transnational R&D investment. Regional centers offer an opportunity to access and disseminate technical expertise, harmonize the regulatory environment for release of new crop varieties and management practices, and prevent redundancy in agricultural research among neighboring countries.

Traditional Approaches

Traditional agricultural assistance that could be combined with the above solutions might include developing and deploying new and existing agricultural technologies; improving water, soil, and land management; and expanding and modernizing transportation, storage, sanitation, and trade infrastructure.

Agricultural Technologies. Although we judge that no breakthrough technological advances to address food problems—on the order of a new green revolution—will be globally deployed by 2025, technology will make important contributions in the years ahead. The global deployment and greater adoption of existing technologies—to include transportation infrastructure, fertilizers, and soil and water conservation techniques—would increase agricultural productivity. Maintaining agricultural commodities on a profitable price plateau will be key to stimulating investment and research in the agricultural sector.

- Emerging next-generation crop varieties are being bred for novel traits, including disease and pest resistance, environmental stress tolerance, and nutritional quality. Some drought-tolerant varieties of corn and rice are near commercial release and many more are in the development phase, according to Western press reporting and academic experts.

- Significant agricultural productivity improvements will require advances in other fields including molecular biology, chemistry, electrical engineering, remote sensing, and computer science. The tools from these fields are not necessarily developed specifically for agriculture, but their application can make improvements in controlling the management of soil, water, crop, and energy inputs to agriculture.

---

[k] Phase-zero operations are pre-conflict operations to reduce the risk of conflict.

Continued Barriers for Genetically Engineered Crops and Biofuels

Regulatory and economic barriers for biotech seeds and biofuels are unlikely to ease during the next 10 years.

- We assess that the use of genetically engineered (GE) seeds will gain greater acceptance in the production of animal feed, nonfood, and industrial crops to 2025. Major global acceptance of GE crops for direct human consumption will continue to meet resistance, however, owing to concerns about health and environmental effects and prohibitive costs in developing countries. Given the expected 85-percent increase in meat demand by 2030, GE crops will almost certainly be used to meet feed demands during this time frame. Corn and oilseeds—the two primary GE food products used and traded widely in the world—account for more than 70 percent of the world's animal feed supplies.

- We judge that biofuel and industrial uses of food crops will grow slowly out to 2025 because of lower oil prices and shifting energy policies. Therefore, biofuel and industrial uses will not be a significant threat to global food security, although such uses could produce local stresses. We assess that public and political support for expanding biofuel production using food crops beyond current levels will wane toward the end of the period. This will be especially true as competing fuels and technologies—including natural gas for transportation use and hybrid and electric vehicles—alter the economic viability of and demand for biofuel. Elevated prices of traditional feed stocks such as corn, sugar, and oilseeds would prompt countries to look for alternatives, such as cassava, and investors and governments would seek to accelerate the development of advanced biofuels.

- Advanced biofuels, including cellulosic ethanol, may be available in larger quantities by 2025, but are not competitive at current oil prices.

Resource Management. We judge that improving the management of natural resources vital to food production, such as soil and water, would strengthen the resilience of communities to reduced food security. Climate-smart agriculture is a practice that employs agricultural conservation solutions, such as no-till farming and planting cover crops, supplemented by agricultural technology solutions like precision agriculture and drip irrigation. These approaches aim to sustainably increase agricultural productivity and incomes, build farmers' resilience to climate change, and reduce greenhouse gas emissions. These techniques also conserve key natural resources.

- Minimal or no-till practices maintain and improve soil water and nutrient storage by reducing the risk of erosion and preserving soil structure. Such practices require less labor and fuel inputs than traditional plow farming; however, these practices generally require the increased use of herbicides and can reduce yields. Mixed cropping, including the use of multipurpose trees and rotations, also can increase soil nutrient availability, reduce erosion, and increase crop yields.

Reserved for Technology Foldout

Back page of technology fold out.

- Today's precision agriculture is suited for large-scale, industrial agriculture practices. Implementing precision agriculture—the use of soil sensors and geolocation technologies for planting, watering, feeding, and harvesting—more widely would require scaling down the technologies to facilitate their use in small plots in the developing world where the greatest potential productivity gains can be made.

- Drip irrigation, despite its higher installation costs, will probably be common in developed countries by 2040 and will be adopted more widely in developing countries as freshwater supplies become scarcer, according to an IC-sponsored study. Regulating the price of water would create incentives for investment and better management of water resources. However, such regulations would come with high political costs—especially in the Middle East—and would not be a viable option for many governments at least through 2025.

Trade Infrastructure. We judge that strengthening the capacity and reliability of trade infrastructure offers a way to improve a region's ability to withstand political and environmental disruptions. Although reliable infrastructure is needed down to the lowest levels to ensure food security for all, three emerging regional corridors will become vital to achieve a major increase in accessible food supplies both locally and globally: Brazil's Northern Export Corridor, the East African Trade Corridor, and the Economic Activity of West African States (ECOWAS) Trade Corridor.

- The greatest expansion in Brazil's agricultural production during the next 10 years is likely to occur in the northern and Amazonian regions. The country will face constraints, however, in getting surplus production to market for export unless major improvements are made in rail, road, and port networks in these regions, according to industry press reporting.

- Increasing the safety, reliability, and interconnectedness of rail and road networks throughout Sub-Saharan Africa, especially in West and East Africa, would pay large dividends. These measures would improve regional trade and help stabilize local and regional prices and supplies year-round in areas with some of the worst chronic food insecurity in the world. In many African countries, shipping food from Europe into African ports is cheaper than moving it a few hundred miles within the continent because of the costs and delays associated with land-based shipment.

- In East Africa, regional transshipment points face severe capacity constraints during the next 10 years.

- Some shipping lines have begun to use North African or European ports as alternative transshipment hubs for West Africa, raising the costs of shipping farther into the interior.

Institutional Capacity. We assess that building the capacity of governments to provide legal, administrative, and regulatory systems for the agricultural and food sectors would increase food security. The effectiveness of public sector institutions in promoting agricultural growth is hampered because many different ministries or agencies operate within the sector, and many public sector institutions are oversized, overly centralized, and staffed by underskilled workers.

- Rather than serving as a main driver of establishing new markets, many governments, especially those in Africa, during the next 10 years are likely to shift toward the role of coordinators that develop and enforce the rules by which private sector participants interact within markets, according to the World

Bank. This change, however, requires considerable public sector capacity to formulate and implement policies that promote market development and coordination. To be successful, public sector institutions must also have the capacity to respond to markets. Although current development strategies provide for increased private sector leadership and a declining role for the public sector, the quality and efficiency of public sector institutions and policies are increasingly important to the emergence of modernized and competitive agriculture.

- Development and implementation of policies affecting the agricultural sector will increasingly depend on ministries and agencies outside of the agricultural ministry, including public finance, trade, natural resource management, and science and technology. Effective communication among the various players will be needed to implement policies. Ministries of agriculture have tended to focus on food production and self-sufficiency; to improve food security, this focus would need to be broadened to include poverty reduction and environmental concerns.

- Improving the capacity of negotiators at regional or global fora, such as the World Trade Organization (WTO), could help countries effectively represent the best short-and long-term needs and concerns of their domestic populations. Donor agencies could provide technical assistance and training to assist negotiators. Such assistance would enable public officials to evaluate potential negotiating positions in categories such as trade, the environment, grades and standards for market entry, intellectual property issues, foreign investment, and negotiating positions with donor agencies.

Implications for the United States

KJ D. Developing creative complements to traditional approaches to improve global food security will take a worldwide effort. Opportunities exist for the United States—already viewed as a leader in promoting global food security—to align with long-standing allies as well as new partners. Some countries offer nontraditional models of how to resolve the inherent tension between goals such as producing more food and conserving water and other natural resources. Emerging economies with growing food security expertise can offer solutions more palatable to countries with low levels of development and technology. Food-insecure countries themselves will also be an important part of the effort; those taking complete or partial ownership of programs designed to build local food security are likely to see more sustainable results.

- Countries will expect the United States to open its domestic markets to foreign producers and continue to encourage the free flow of fertilizers, energy, and food-related services and equipment under global trade agreements.

- Many governments will seek guidance from the United States and others on how to manage competing priorities, such as keeping urban food prices down while also ensuring that farmers have incentives to produce, or finding ways that countries can better tap into underutilized water resources while protecting the current ecosystem or environment.

Improving Agricultural Growth Management and Investments.

Historical attempts by governments to offer large, low-cost tracts of public land for foreign or domestic development have mostly met with failure. Land deals of tens or hundreds of thousands of acres often are too cumbersome to manage, lack necessary capital and expertise, and focus more on short-term gains rather than long-term sustainability, especially when land rents are low.

- The policies and market conditions that small-scale commercial farmers need to thrive are very different from those that are required for subsistence farmers. Therefore, government policies that treat these two categories as separate entities and provide for the unique needs of each are likely to encourage greater resilience and agricultural growth, according to academics.

The development of greater commercialization in agriculture will partially depend on revising land-tenure laws and ownership/use regulations. US and international academic research shows that secure land tenure is an important factor affecting agricultural technology use by small farmers because it provides incentives for investment to enhance the productivity of the land and reduces the risk to farmers.

- Most countries in Africa lack land tenure laws that are necessary to create sustainable commercial opportunities in agriculture, including legal security of land owners and users, and limits to property transfers, according to an Africa-focused research institution.

- Effective land tenure reforms include those that: 1) clarify rights of land users; 2) recognize and expand rights for women—who comprise the majority of the world's farmers—to use and transfer property; 3) manage potentially conflicting claims of property users effectively—including between pastoralists and farmers; 4) create more effective dispute resolution processes; and 5) recognize communal land ownership.

Higher Expectations

Most countries and aid organizations will almost certainly turn to the United States for leadership and assistance to improve global food security. As a major source of agricultural technology and innovation, the United States will be expected to continue to develop and share advanced food technologies. However, many developing countries are looking to cooperate with other developing countries on agricultural technology issues because of regional dietary preferences and because some developing countries have made agricultural advances based on small-scale water, land, and crop-management practices. This well positions these countries to gain greater global influence through their agricultural research programs.

- As the world's largest provider of food aid, the United States will be expected to continue to support food development efforts and provide assistance during local or regional emergencies.

Developing countries will expect the United States to adapt its agricultural development operations to better suit these countries' limited abilities to use first-world technologies, especially in areas that lack reliable electricity and maintenance capacity. Emerging markets which have developed innovative and self-sustaining agricultural research potential during the past 30 years, are also poised to provide these new techniques in the developing world.

- Food security improvement efforts designed to slowly and deliberately work to develop predominant subsistence-farming practices into small- and mid-sized commercial farms are more likely to be effective at increasing food security than rapid investment in large-scale, industrial agriculture.

Working With Partners
Several traditional partners of the United States with robust expertise and capabilities in improving agricultural production and food security would probably be willing to engage with the United States and the international community on a greater scale.

- Reducing the number of people facing poverty and food insecurity will almost certainly remain one of the key development concerns as countries seek to develop their post-2015 Millennium Development Goals. Although almost 40 countries have met the goal of halving the number of people suffering from poverty and hunger, progress has been uneven: Sub-Saharan Africa trails the rest of the world. It is the only region that has seen the number of people living in extreme poverty rise steadily, from 290 million in 1990 to 414 million in 2010.

- As of May 2014, 127 billionaires had pledged to provide half their fortunes to charity—many to agricultural and food security projects—when they die. This will create a huge windfall for many nongovernmental organizations (NGOs) and foundations that currently might not have the capacity to fully use and handle such a large influx of funding. Helping to build their capacities now could prevent bottlenecks and more quickly generate positive results in reducing poverty and food insecurity as funding becomes available.

Annex A
Research Used for This Assessment

In May 2008, the National Intelligence Council (NIC) produced the National Intelligence Assessment, **National Security Implications of Global Climate Change to 2030**, (NIA 2008-01). The key finding was that climate change alone is unlikely to trigger state failure through 2030, but the effects of climate change—reduced water availability, degraded agriculture production, damage to infrastructure, and changes in disease patterns—will worsen existing problems such as poverty, social tensions, environmental degradation, ineffectual leadership, and weak political institutions. The NIC has subsequently published reports on global water security and health issues.

To produce this Assessment, the NIC commissioned six external unclassified efforts to explore global food security. **Global Food Security: Key Drivers**, (NICR 2012-05, 1 February 2012) outlined the findings of a conference on food security. **Global Food Security: Market Forces and Selected Case Studies**, (NICR 2012-23, 10 May 2012) explored market forces that will affect food security. **Global Food Security: Emerging Technologies to 2040**, (NICR 2012-30, 28 Aug 2012) identified emerging, potentially breakthrough technologies for agriculture (see foldout on page 15). **Natural Resources in 2020, 2030, and 2040: Implications for the United States**, (NICR 2013-05, 25 July 2013) focused on supply and demand for food (see Annex C), water, energy, and minerals out to 2040 and was used to support the NIC's **Global Trends 2030** project. **The Future of Indian Ocean and South China Sea Fisheries: Implications for the United States**, (NICR 2013-38, 30 July 2013) focused on the fisheries of the Indian Ocean and South China Sea (see Annex F). The sixth report was an unpublished evaluation of global food security and implications for US national security—completed in April 2013—that evaluated food security in 36 countries as well as seven major agricultural commodities.

The year 2040 was selected as the target endpoint for these research efforts. We selected this endpoint to enable us to consider longer-term effects of climate change, growing populations, continued global economic development, and emerging food technologies. However, the data referenced in all of the NIC's external research efforts covers a wide range of dates, some as far out as 2050.

This page has been intentionally left blank.

Annex B
Methodological Note

Our approach to analyzing the risk of increasing food insecurity in the period from 2015-2025 required two distinct ways of measuring food security on a global scale. First, we used an openly available food-security risk index to establish the current risk of food security. We then overlaid that with a simple binary model with several projected risk factors that were mutually exclusive—both from the current risk index and each other. These indicators fell into three broad categories: food-supply disruptions, purchasing power, and counterproductive government policies. When the future risk indicators were present within a certain limit—generally above or below the global average for most factors—they were recorded as a 1, and when not present, were recorded as a 0. Each indicator was ranked equally with no weight assigned because of the varying applicability of each indicator to each country. Countries exhibiting an established number of present risk factors were deemed at risk of worsening food insecurity. Our analysis excluded countries that had a population of less than 500,000 because of a lack of data.

The IC examines state stability as a critical part of determining potential threats to US interests. The IC considers water, food, energy availability, and other factors in making such assessments. It is difficult to discern the impact of one factor on food security because in most cases multiple factors are at play.

To address how individuals and societies react to limited natural resources, the IC solicits the views of governmental and nongovernmental regional experts and develops an analytical synthesis to arrive at its judgment regarding likely developments. A better understanding and explanation of human behavior in response to environmental stresses, to include shocks stemming from environmental problems, would enhance the integration of social, economic (infrastructure, agriculture, and manufacturing), military, environmental, and political models. In the interim, assessing the future of a society's development will be a scenario-driven exercise and an imprecise science. The use of outside experts is critical to our success.

This page has been intentionally left blank.

Annex C
Food Supply-and-Demand Outlook and Key Agricultural Commodities

Food Supply-and-Demand Outlook[l]

Overall global food supply will keep pace with demand during the next 10 years. Demand for agricultural products almost certainly will remain strong, but will expand at a slower rate compared with the past decade because of the declining population growth-rate and more gradual population growth in emerging markets. However, expansion of agricultural production will probably also slow during the next 10 years because increases in the amount of area cultivated and yield growth rates are likely to be smaller than in previous years. This is likely to limit the rise in stock-to-use ratios[m] through at least 2025 and increase the risk of price volatility because some major producing and consuming countries face challenges in rebuilding their foodstocks.

Global agricultural production is unlikely to be able to maintain the 2.1-percent annual growth seen during the previous decade because of higher costs of production, growing resource constraints, and increasing environmental pressures. The latest OECD-FAO World Agricultural Outlook for 2014-2023 projects a relatively consistent global rate of growth in production—about 1.5 percent per year—during the next 10 years. This projected growth rate would just keep pace with the OECD-FAO's projected growth in demand for agricultural products in developing countries, but the rate would outpace expected global population growth by 1 percent per year. Demand is expected to grow at the highest rates—2.5 percent in Sub-Saharan Africa, for example—where existing technologies offer good potential for increasing yields.

Average prices of agricultural commodities are expected to decline in real terms after peaks in the previous decade, according to the OECD-FAO, but macroeconomic factors, resource constraints, and changing climates are likely to produce price spikes and volatility in some commodities. Trade restrictions and weather-driven production shortfalls are likely to be the primary causes of price surges during this time frame. Other factors likely to exacerbate volatility are biofuel policies—which could tie agricultural prices more closely to oil prices—and, in the medium to long term, climate change.

During the next 10 years, the demand for particular foods—such as meat and dairy products—will grow faster than the demand for most other agricultural products because of the dietary preferences of an expanding middle class. Population growth will probably account for most of the increases in direct human consumption per capita of basic grains, such as wheat and rice, during this same time period. As incomes increase, consumption of traditional basic staples usually expands to include an increased

---

[l] This Annex was extracted from the report on Natural Resources as well as other sources (See Annex A).
[m] The stocks-to-use ratio is a convenient measure of supply-and-demand interrelationships of commodities. The stocks-to-use ratio indicates the level of carryover stock for any given commodity as a percentage of the total demand or use.

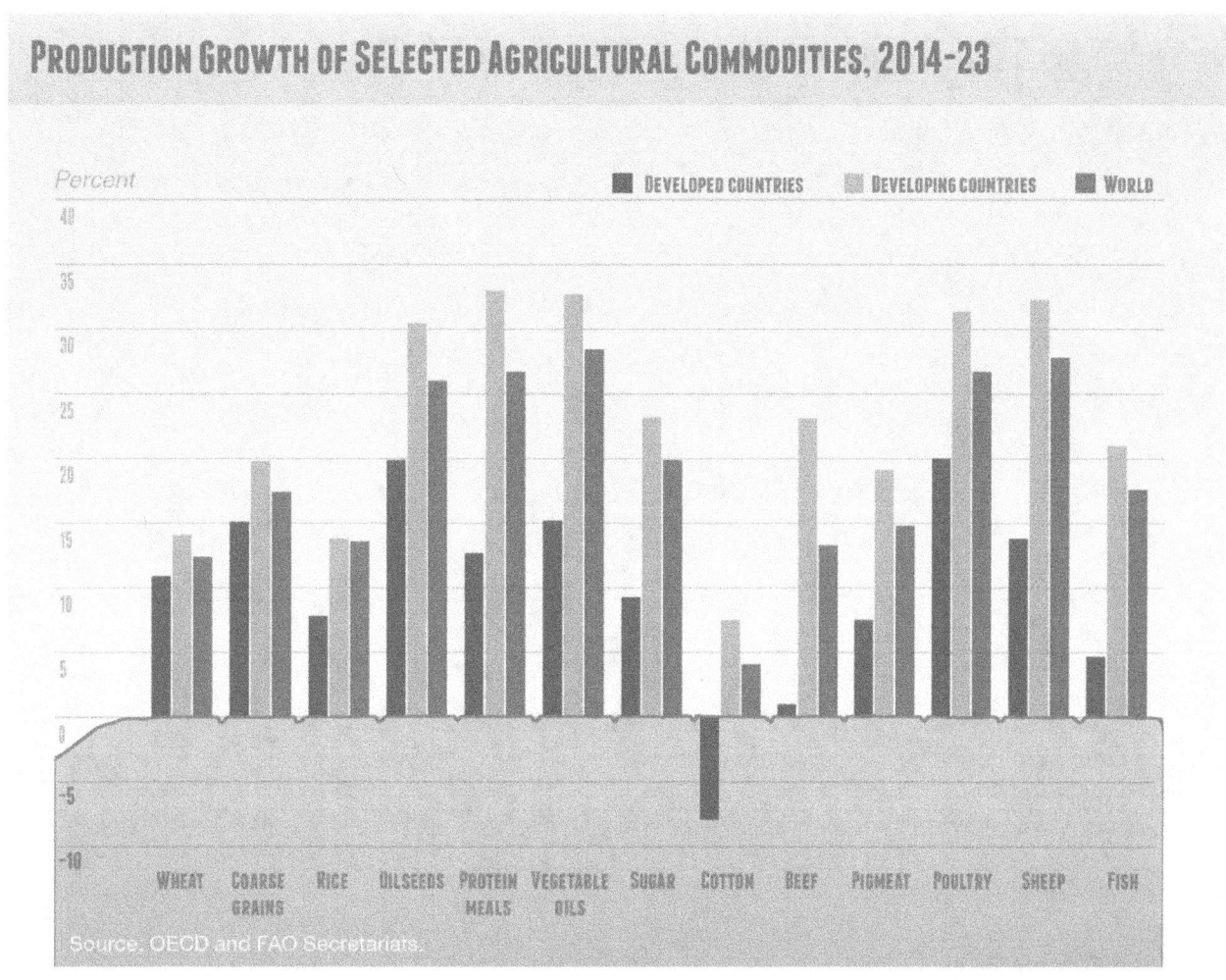

PRODUCTION GROWTH OF SELECTED AGRICULTURAL COMMODITIES, 2014-23

Percent

DEVELOPED COUNTRIES   DEVELOPING COUNTRIES   WORLD

Categories: WHEAT, COARSE GRAINS, RICE, OILSEEDS, PROTEIN MEALS, VEGETABLE OILS, SUGAR, COTTON, BEEF, PIGMEAT, POULTRY, SHEEP, FISH

Source: OECD and FAO Secretariats.

variety of foods. For example, increased rice consumption per capita in Africa, North America, and Europe will be offset partially by decreased per capita rice consumption in Asian countries, such as China. Many countries will rely more on the international market to fill their food demand as a growing middle class demands less traditional foods.

Higher demand for processed foods, animal feed, and biofuel will drive rapid growth in production of coarse grains and oilseeds. Both of these classes of commodities might experience a doubling in globally traded supplies during the next 10 years, according to the US Department of Agriculture (USDA) and FAO. Developing countries will probably benefit from this trend because agricultural production growth will be highest in developing countries for these commodities, while the growth in production of these commodities in major developed countries will remain steady or slowly decline, according to the FAO. Corn and soybeans will experience some of the largest growth in production and consumption; vegetable oils, such as palm oil, will continue to experience significantly increased trade volumes on the international market.

CHANGES IN CONSUMPTION OF SELECTED COMMODITIES, 2014-23

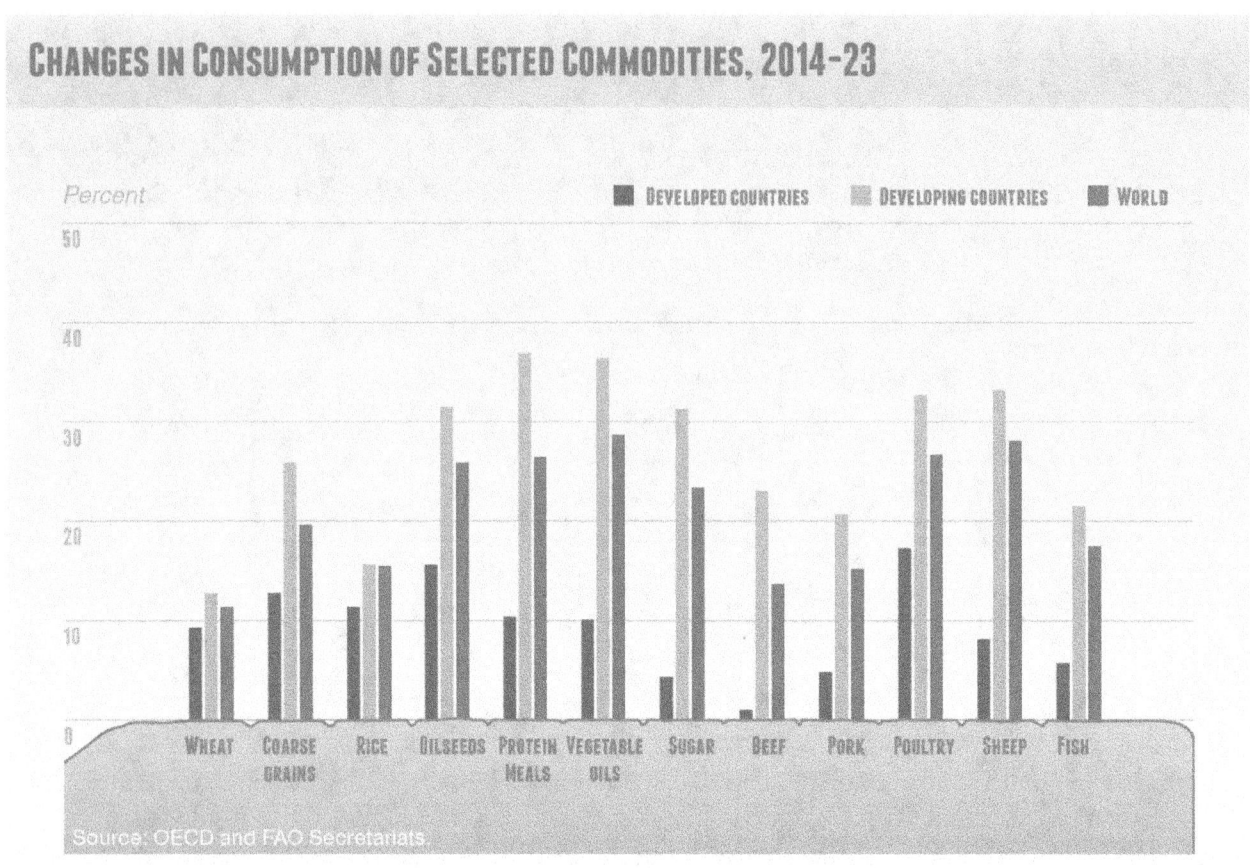

Percent

DEVELOPED COUNTRIES · DEVELOPING COUNTRIES · WORLD

Source: OECD and FAO Secretariats.

Key Food Commodities

Six key agricultural products and commodities—wheat, rice, coarse grains, oil crops, sugar crops, and fish—will comprise the majority of global trade and calories for the greatest number of people throughout the world. In many countries, accessibility of these foods is based on political considerations. The alteration of global or local production or distribution of these commodities has the potential to create instability in countries important to US national security. The majority of the chart data in this section are attributable to the *OECD-FAO World Agricultural Outlook 2014-2023*.

Wheat

Supply. World wheat production is expected to just keep pace with global population growth because the growth in the amount of wheat produced per acre has been slowing, with increases during the next 10 years probably at about 1 percent in contrast to a 1.5 percent during this previous decade. The use of technology has not reversed this trend, in part because genetically engineered varieties are not commercially accepted. Most global wheat production is rain-fed, especially in major exporting countries, making the market for wheat more vulnerable to weather conditions than for many other crops. Major producers are in water-stressed environments vulnerable to extreme weather. These trends will probably put upward pressure on wheat prices and on existing supplies. A further potential supply disruption

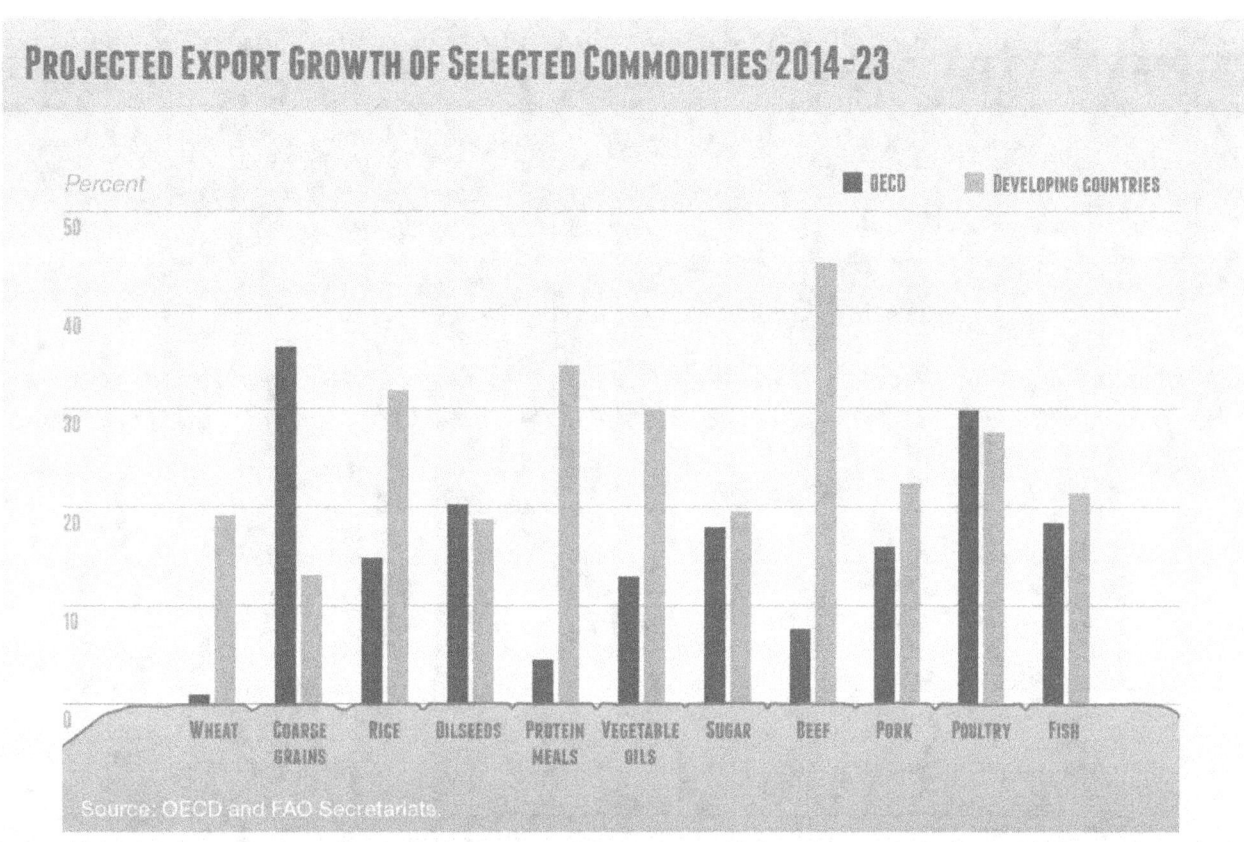

PROJECTED EXPORT GROWTH OF SELECTED COMMODITIES 2014-23

Percent

■ OECD   ▓ DEVELOPING COUNTRIES

Source: OECD and FAO Secretariats

might occur if the disease Ug99 stem rust[n] arrives in South Asia, which might occur in next few years.

Demand. Wheat is expected to remain a commodity predominately used for human consumption because it is often less economical to use as an animal feed, and it will remain the staple food grain for the most number of countries. The growing demand for wheat is expected to outstrip domestic production in Asia as a result of population growth and the dietary preferences of an expanding middle class, but the amount of wheat consumed in North America and Europe will probably remain the same or decline per capita. Demand also will probably be influenced by corn prices because wheat can be substituted for corn in animal feed when corn prices rise. Wheat already is the primary feed grain in countries that produce more wheat supplies than corn.

---

[n] Ug99 is a fungus that affects grains, such as wheat and barley, and can completely destroy a crop. Most wheat varieties world-wide are susceptible.

28

ARABLE LAND EXPANSION AND YIELD GROWTH IN SELECTED CROPS, 2014-23

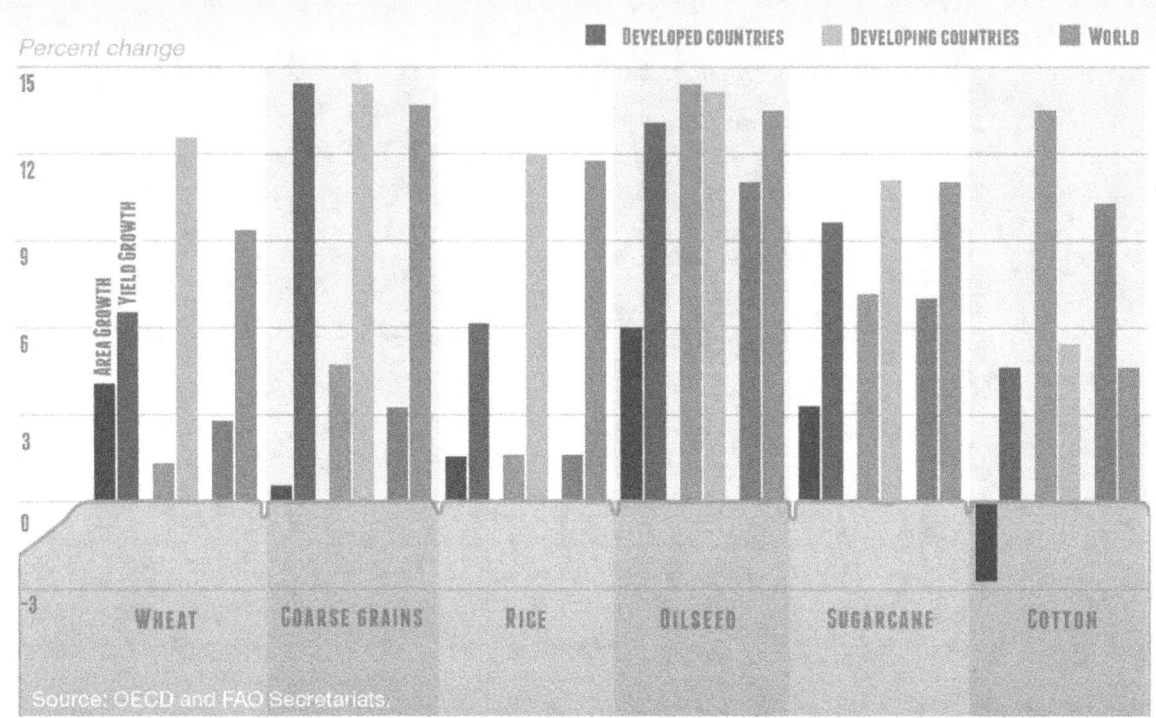

Source: OECD and FAO Secretariats.

Rice

Supply. World rice production is projected to grow about 1.2 percent per year during the next 10 years—a significant slowdown from the 2.2 percent growth recorded in the previous 10 years because the amount of the world's land used for growing rice is mostly stagnating or declining. Nevertheless, growth in rice production will outpace population growth. Virtually all of the expected increase in production stems from gains in productivity, rather than an expansion of the land devoted to growing rice. However, in Africa and some Asian countries, which still hold large tracts of uncultivated land and abundant water, the amount of land used for growing rice is slowly increasing. Because most rice production relies on irrigation, downturns in production caused by seasonal weather are less extreme, and many rice-producing countries also have more than one rice crop per year. Anticipated changes in rainfall patterns due to climate change are expected to affect rice yields, but experts do not yet know the magnitude and direction of this effect. However, many rice-producing countries face water-stressed environments, including with upstream dam construction, that threaten long-term rice production.

Demand. In Asia, where much of the rice produced is consumed domestically, per capita rice consumption is expected to rise only marginally or decline, because diets are diversifying away from traditional staple grains. On the other hand, per capita rice consumption will keep growing in African countries, where rice is gaining relative importance as a major food staple. Rice imports are expected to increase in Africa because demand will probably continue to outpace production. Most rice consumers in East Asia prefer local rice varieties, making the rice production sector one of the most protected domestic industries in these countries. Shocks to local production can have large effects on access to rice. Government policies—such as rice procurement policies and export bans—could again cause broader fluctuation in the global rice market because only a small percentage of global rice production is traded and only a few countries export the crop. The price of rice spiked during the 2008 food crisis because of the collapse in confidence in the rice market and the subsequent imposition of export controls, even though global rice production had increased from the previous year. Importers began panic buying and the price tripled in only a few months.

Coarse Grains

Supply. The production of coarse grains°—such as corn, barley, and sorghum—is projected to grow 17 percent during the next 10 years because of expanded acreage and yield growth increases. This is a slower rate than in the past; as a result, prices for all coarse grains will probably remain stable. Worldwide, most coarse grains are used for animal feed, suggesting that supply shortages might cause price increases across a variety of foods. Corn yields, particularly in developing countries, will probably be hurt the most by climate change in the coming years. Corn is also a water-intensive crop and will therefore almost certainly be adversely affected by water shortages.

Demand. The expansion of livestock production in feed-deficit countries continues to be the principal driver of growth in coarse-grain consumption, especially in middle-income countries. The additional demand for biofuel production drives the demand for coarse grains—primarily corn—in developed countries. Key growth markets include East Asia, parts of North America, and countries in Africa and the Middle East that will use coarse grains as animal feed and for malting-barley. Continued reliance on corn as a biofuel feedstock in the near and medium term will increase demand and make corn prices more closely linked to oil prices, which traditionally have displayed greater volatility than food prices.

Oil Crops and Their Derivatives

Supply. The production of oil crops will probably rise faster than the production of any other group of food commodities during the next 10 years because of large available land expansion of these crops and new technologies. Oilseed production—dominated by soybeans and rapeseed (canola)—is projected to grow 2 percent per year with planted acreage expanding 11 percent and yields increasing by 14 percent. Most of these oilseeds are crushed to produce protein meals and vegetable oils. Seventy percent of soybeans, which comprise about 60 percent of all oilseeds produced, are consumed as animal feed. Production of palm oil, the other major vegetable oil, will increase about 2.9 percent per year; most of this growth will occur in Southeast Asia. Planted acreage for corn and oilseeds will remain competitive because the two share the same growing season and desired soil types. Because so few countries are able to produce oil crops in sufficient quantities to meet the rising demands of their populations, volatility in global markets for these crops can have significant effects on the prices of these goods. Although state instability will probably not occur in the main producing countries, external shocks, such as droughts, might cause short-term price fluctuations.

° Coarse grains generally refer to all grains that are not wheat or rice, and include corn, barley, sorghum, and millet.

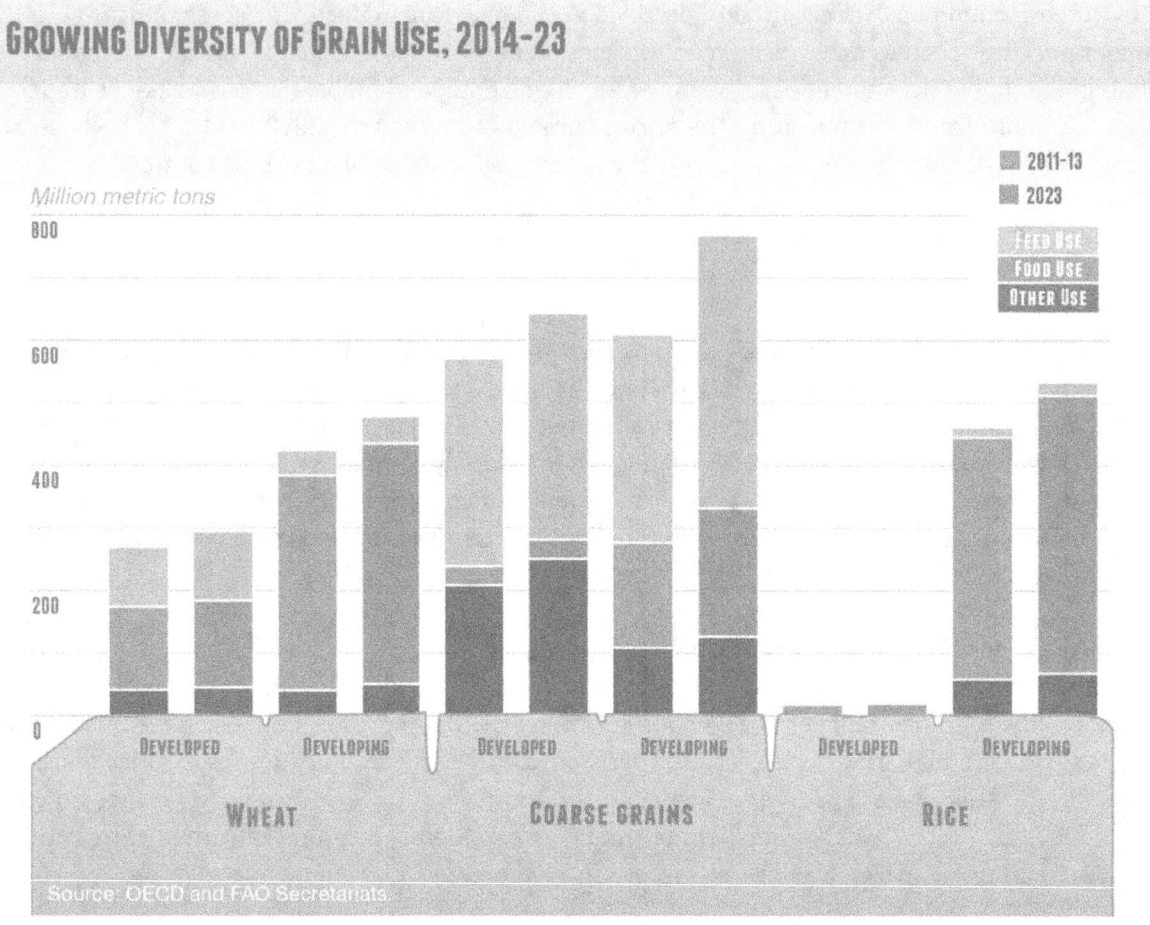

GROWING DIVERSITY OF GRAIN USE, 2014-23

Million metric tons

Legend: 2011-13 · 2023 · FEED USE · FOOD USE · OTHER USE

WHEAT: DEVELOPED, DEVELOPING
COARSE GRAINS: DEVELOPED, DEVELOPING
RICE: DEVELOPED, DEVELOPING

Source: OECD and FAO Secretariats.

Demand. Vegetable oils are an essential component of most people's diets in almost all countries worldwide. The demand for oilseed protein meal as an animal feed will be mainly driven by increased demand for poultry, pork, and milk, while the food and biodiesel sectors will dominate demand for vegetable oil. The bulk of biodiesel demand will be driven by national mandates because biodiesel fuel is not expected to be economically viable compared to diesel fuel. Rising per capita income in many developing countries is expected to lead to a 1.3-percent annual increase in per capita vegetable oil consumption; consumption of oil crops is expected to remain stable in developed countries.

Sugar

Supply. Global sugar production is projected to increase by 1.9 percent during the next 10 years. Most increases in sugar production will result from increased yields rather than an expansion of acreage devoted to the crop because the sugar sector is capital-intensive with very high fixed costs. Most of the production will originate from countries that produce sugar cane rather than sugar beets.

Demand. Growth in consumption of sugar for food will continue to be dominated by the sugar-deficit regions of Africa and Asia. Developing countries—driven by rising incomes, urbanization, and growing populations—will continue to display the fastest growth in demand. Health concerns, often associated with high sugar consumption, in developed and some developing countries, might reduce the demand for sugar in the medium-to-longer term. By 2025, about 30 percent of the global sugarcane crop might be used in ethanol production, up from 15 percent currently.

Fish

Supply. World fishery production is expected to be 17 percent higher during the next 10 years, led by gains in aquaculture output. Developing countries will account for almost all of the projected production growth, garnering about 84 percent of total production. Overfishing is an ongoing concern. A number of individual countries and international groups have taken steps to reduce overfishing, and some progress toward recovery has been reported in certain fisheries. However, of the 600 fish stocks monitored by the FAO, 52 percent are fished at renewable capacity while 25 percent are overexploited, depleted, or in recovery.

Demand. Rising demand for fish will be led by developing countries, especially in Asia. The fish will be used primarily for direct human consumption. The driving force behind this increase will be rising incomes and urbanization, increased production, and improved distribution channels. Sub-Saharan Africa will become more dependent on fish imports as demand for fish from a growing population outstrips fish production. However, because of higher costs than previous domestic catches, fish imports are unlikely to fill the growing gap between supply and demand. Food security will decline because the population will lack sufficient fish proteins and micronutrients.

Annex D
Food, Water, and Energy Nexus

The availability of water and energy will have far-reaching effects on global food security during the next 10 years. Declining per capita availability of natural resources will increase the importance of a "nexus approach" to managing water, food, and energy. There is an inextricable link among the three sectors and actions in one sector affect one or both of the others. A nexus approach facilitates the development of policies and investments that exploit interdependencies across the water, energy, and food sectors by considering the needs, uses, and consequences of development in all three sectors concurrently. The approach enables planners to make informed resource trade-off decisions rather than suffer the unintended, adverse, consequences often associated with a failure to integrate sectors. Such an approach is particularly important in view of the effects of climate change and pollution.

Food security is strongly linked to water availability. World agriculture consumes 71 percent of the world's water, placing this resource at the heart of the nexus approach. Excessive water waste results largely from poor management and the perception of water as an infinite resource. The infrastructure and energy costs associated with water supply and treatment are largely, if not wholly, subsidized by governments. As a result, the declining availability of water and the cost of providing it are not factored directly into food pricing. For example, several of the top 10 food exporters are water-scarce regions that indirectly export their dwindling water resources as "virtual water.[p]" Biofuels are another example: although providing seemingly "inexpensive" energy, biofuels are only inexpensive because the full cost of water is not factored into their price. The use of biofuels—primarily ethanol and biodiesel—for transportation has grown rapidly worldwide. According to many government, academic, and industry experts, today's biofuels provide little environmental benefit and consume or displace food crops.

The following examples illustrate the complex connections between the water, energy, and food sectors:

- Reservoirs and rivers used for hydroelectric generation also are often used to supply agricultural irrigation. However, downstream irrigation schemes can suffer if water is held back in reservoirs to ensure steady supplies of energy, while large outtakes for irrigation water upstream can reduce the water needed to power hydroelectric turbines.

- Intensive water use supports all facets of the energy sector, including resource extraction, processing, electric power generation, and storage and transport. While the US energy sector has high water-use requirements, the water sector can have high energy requirements.

- Oil production consumes 1 to 14 gallons of water per gallon of oil, and coal-washing requires 20 to 40 gallons per ton of coal washed.

---

[p] *Virtual water* is the water used (or consumed) in the development or production of a good or commodity, typically agricultural products.

WATER-ENERGY-FOOD NEXUS

A nexus approach to management that considered the needs, uses, and consequences of development in all three sectors together would probably lead to a more optimal allocation of resources, improved economic efficiency, lower environment and livelihood impacts, and better economic development conditions. Below are some of the linkages, but not an exhaustive list.

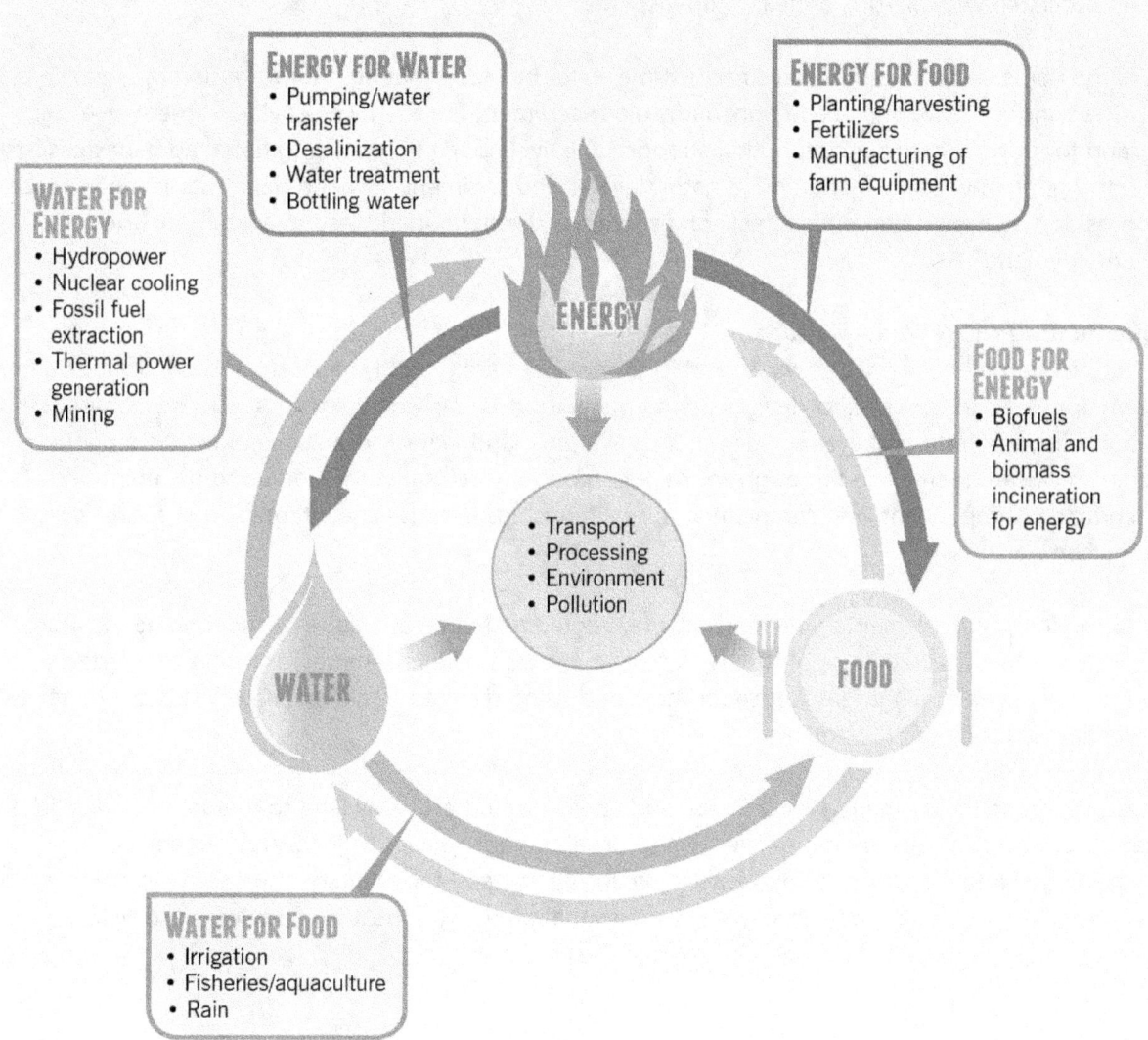

ENERGY FOR WATER
- Pumping/water transfer
- Desalinization
- Water treatment
- Bottling water

ENERGY FOR FOOD
- Planting/harvesting
- Fertilizers
- Manufacturing of farm equipment

WATER FOR ENERGY
- Hydropower
- Nuclear cooling
- Fossil fuel extraction
- Thermal power generation
- Mining

FOOD FOR ENERGY
- Biofuels
- Animal and biomass incineration for energy

ENERGY

- Transport
- Processing
- Environment
- Pollution

WATER

FOOD

WATER FOR FOOD
- Irrigation
- Fisheries/aquaculture
- Rain

- The quality of water affects not only water itself, but also food and energy. Water pollution stemming from the energy sector, including processing and extraction waste or spills, sometimes renders water unusable for agriculture, fishing, and human consumption unless the water is highly treated.

- Flood-irrigation techniques often cause soil salinization, which can lead to a reduction in crop cultivation because the useable soil area is reduced and yields are lower, jeopardizing food security.

- Energy-intensive desalination of sea water for human consumption increases local ocean salinity and is associated with die-offs of near-shore fisheries.

- Large dams and resultant reservoirs consume water by redistributing it for irrigation projects and increasing evaporation. In addition, dams block sediment flows, which provide nutrient-rich soil and land for downstream agriculture that supports the livelihoods of many traditional agro-pastoralists[q] in developing countries. Disruption of natural water and sediment flow and distribution can increase erosion and have detrimental effects on fisheries and other aquatic resources that provide employment.

Implementing the Nexus Approach

Institutions that manage energy, water, and food resources are typically separate and do not take a multi-system approach toward project development. Many food, water, and energy issues have competitive relationships, e.g. industrial uses versus water quality and land/water/ocean sovereignty. Competing relationships can be managed through coordination of all systems involved. In addition, many dependent, co-dependent, and complementary relationships improve the integration of food, water, and energy components.

- Examples of complementary relationships that could be fostered include conducting aquaculture in flooded rice fields (dual use of water); burning biomass waste for energy resources and fertilizer; using biomass waste as a nutrient source for food; and using rivers to transport materials between terrestrial marine environments.

A nexus approach to managing food, water, and energy would probably lead to a more optimal allocation of resources, improved economic efficiency and development, fewer lost jobs, and less severe environmental effects. Often the opposite is occurring: states—for a variety of reasons—subsidize food, water, or energy, or pursue development strategies that are not the best for an overall ecosystem.

---

[q] Small-scale farmers whose livelihoods depend on a mixture of herding and crop raising.

Nexus Example

Not all linkages are shown in the diagram.

Annex E
Food Safety

As the world faces significant food security problems, food safety is likely to gain even more prominence as a global issue through 2025 and require increased collaboration among nations. The continued globalization and diversification of the food market and greater public demand for health protection will increase the global focus on food safety. Major food exporters will most likely adopt more stringent food safety standards to remain competitive in global markets. Stricter international food safety regulations, however, will inhibit the ability of small-scale producers to penetrate international markets. Such restrictions will probably ultimately contribute to higher food prices because of the added costs of meeting the regulations. Food safety scandals might cause international tensions, boycotts, and political and structural changes.

Highly publicized food scandals in recent years have shifted the global emphasis beyond the price and basic quality of food to food safety and animal health concerns. As emerging countries play a larger role in expanding world agricultural trade, we assess that these countries will be pressed to improve their food-safety programs.

The proposed tightening of food-safety regulations will probably generate controversy as food producers seek to meet growing demands, and policymakers in developing countries struggle to balance food-safety modernization with preserving traditional activities.

The globalization of the food market, which increases the exportation and importation of food products among countries, poses new food-safety risks from emerging diseases, re-introduces previously controlled risks, and might foster the spread of contaminated food across wider geographical areas. Food contamination incidents will almost certainly be more difficult to prevent in the coming years, even with significant improvements to national food-safety regulations. The greatest challenge arising from food contamination is that the use of unconventional contaminants could go undetected until populations report significant adverse health effects.

- Consumer-ready foods (seafood, fresh fruits and vegetables, and processed foods), particularly those originating from low- to middle-income countries, are the foods most likely to be contaminated. The dietary preferences of growing middle classes in developing countries increase the demand for fresh products; such demand is predominantly being met by countries with underdeveloped food-safety programs. Food contamination with microbial pathogens is still one of the greatest food-safety risks causing human diseases, although other contaminants, such as veterinary drugs and pesticide residues, are gaining more global attention.

- Seafood is likely to be the source of a major contamination incident in future years, given that aquaculture (farm fishing) is the fastest-growing sector of the global food production industry and that aquaculture farms are not uniformly regulated. Common aquaculture practices result in food contamination caused by excessive antibiotics and pesticides and other chemicals that are used to prevent the fish from getting diseases and parasites.

We judge that growing food demand through 2020 will perpetuate and possibly increase the economically motivated adulteration (EMA) of food products. Intentional food contamination incidents motivated by economic gain will be a rising threat and could spread food-safety fears more broadly than accidental contamination or terrorist threats to the food supply. The increasing global demand for certain food products, particularly processed foods, will most likely result in the illegal adulteration of food items by profit-seeking individuals.

- Although EMA aims to inflate profits by fraudulent means—rather than harm people—we anticipate that serious public health consequences will result from EMA and that the incidence of EMA of food products is likely to increase.

- Difficulties in testing food for safety will increase with the new and emerging contaminants posed by EMA and other threats. The current food-safety testing market is dominated by pathogen testing due to the high prevalence of pathogens in food contamination, with meat and poultry accounting for the major share in food testing by type. We expect that, because of time and resource constraints, the traditional regulatory practices and existing detection methods for food contaminants will not be feasible to test for all potential contaminents that could make their way into food sources.

Annex F
The South China Sea and Indian Ocean Fisheries

Stresses in Indian Ocean (IO) and South China Sea (SCS) fisheries might undermine the internal stability of some countries as well as bilateral and regional relations. The wild fisheries that provide an important dietary staple and livelihoods to many of the 4 billion people living around these fisheries are at risk of exhaustion. Looking to 2020 and beyond to 2040, it will become more difficult to balance rising demand from growing populations and economies with increasing pressure on supplies stemming from overexploitation, pollution, habitat destruction, and climate change. As a result, some wild fisheries in the region will probably close down. Aquaculture (farm fishing) in or around the coasts of the IO and SCS is growing quickly and in some cases offsetting the declining output of wild fisheries.

Fisheries provide an important dietary staple and livelihood to many of the 2.49 billion people of the Indian Ocean (IO) coast and some 1.87 billion people living around the South China Sea in eight southeastern Asian countries, Taiwan, and three Chinese provinces. Fisheries also constitute a key economic resource for many coastal communities.

- Sub-Saharan Africa and South Asia, the two regions of the world projected to experience some of the heaviest population growth over the next 40 years, at least partially border on the Indian Ocean. These marine waters will be relied upon more intensely in coming decades to meet the growing demand for food.

- In 2010—the year for which the most recent data are available—roughly 14.6 percent of the world's total ocean catch came from IO waters, showcasing the IO's growing importance as a lynchpin of both regional—and, increasingly, global—food security. Populations in Egypt, Malaysia, Mozambique, Seychelles, Tanzania, and Thailand get at least one-fifth of their animal protein by consuming fish, while populations in Bangladesh, Comoros, Indonesia, Maldives, and Sri Lanka receive more than half of their animal protein from fish.

- The countries bordering the SCS—Brunei, Cambodia, China, Indonesia, Malaysia, the Philippines, Thailand, and Vietnam—rank among the top fish-producing and -consuming countries in the world in terms of both marine catch and aquaculture. Many people in these countries depend on the fishing industry for both food security and their incomes. According to the FAO, the average daily seafood consumption per person among the coastal states was almost double the global average. Further, three of the top five fishery commodity-exporting nations also hail from the region (China, Thailand, and Vietnam).

Total wild fish capture in the IO and SCS has risen substantially since the 1970s, but in 1999 it began to plateau or even decline for some species. Aquaculture in or around the shores of both the IO and SCS is growing fast and in some cases offsetting the declining output of wild fisheries.

- The health of fisheries in both the IO and SCS is difficult to assess based on total production, which varies slightly from year to year, and data on catches are also frequently inadequate. Total capture from global marine fisheries has remained relatively stable recently, but it trended upward from 64.7 million tons in 2003 to 70.8 million tons in 2013. The total national wild fish catch of some countries in the region can include significant amounts of fish harvested outside coastal waters and the 200 nautical-mile Exclusive Economic Zone (EEZ). In some cases, catches come from beyond the IO or SCS entirely. Despite the appearance of relative stability in the composition of the catch by species and distribution by country, some fishing areas and the types of fish caught have been changing markedly in recent years. Fish size has been steadily decreasing and mature fish are increasingly scarce. Most of the commercially important fish species in both bodies of water have been overfished.

- The rise of marine aquaculture is an important trend throughout the region, with the potential to reduce the strain on wild fish stocks. Bangladesh, Burma, Egypt, India, Indonesia, and Thailand ranked among the world's top ten aquaculture producers in 2010. Those countries combined to farm 11.3 million tons of fish in 2010—roughly the same amount as the total tonnage of fish harvested from the IO's wild-capture fisheries that year. In 2013, China's aquaculture production constituted more than double that of wild fisheries by weight and about 62 percent of total world production.

Looking to 2020 and beyond to 2040, the dual challenges of rising demand from growing populations and economies—colliding with increasing pressures on supply stemming from overexploitation, pollution, habitat destruction, and climate change—will impose serious pressures on fisheries. Total production[r] in 2020 in the IO and SCS will probably be somewhat less to only slightly more than recent production. IO fisheries are at risk of continued overexploitation, a trend that might lead to the outright collapse of some fisheries in the region. The ability of SCS fisheries to accommodate mounting demand is also in doubt.

- The FAO has reported that of 47 IO fish species with sufficient available data to evaluate the condition of those species' wild fish-stocks, 41 were judged to be either "moderate-full" exploited or "full-overexploited." The status of most IO fish species is reported by FAO as "unknown," due to inaccurate reporting or lack of reporting altogether.

- Most rich fishing environments, such as shallow reefs and shoals, in the SCS have already been exploited to their limit or beyond, leaving few relatively underexploited areas. Areas of the SCS might have the potential to support more intensive fishing, but data on those fisheries are unclear, and the technological impediments to harvesting fish far below the surface efficiently may still pose a challenge. In addition, available analyses suggest that climate change could engender substantial shifts in catch sizes and locations by mid-century.

- Coastal and marine areas are among the most vulnerable of all environments to global climate change. The projected effects of global warming include rising sea levels, stronger tropical cyclones, larger storm surges, increasing sea surface temperatures, and growing acidification of surface waters. Climate change will also interact in complex ways with other stressors on marine systems, such as overfishing, habitat destruction, and marine pollution. Significant portions of the IO and SCS are already among the world's marine ecosystems most highly affected by climate change.

---

[r] Total production is often expressed in "landings"—that part of the fish catch that is put ashore and typically measured in tons.

Stresses in the IO and SCS fisheries might undermine the internal stability of some countries as well as bilateral and regional relations. Given other concerns about stability in the region (sovereignty issues, exploitation of oil and natural gas resources, and freedom of navigation), fisheries will probably remain a secondary matter for US national security. In places where competition for fish overlaps with maritime sovereignty, contending claims to fisheries will continue to exacerbate bilateral and regional tensions.

- Poor countries with high levels of seafood consumption are already facing the loss of many jobs owing to the collapse of in-shore fisheries, though aquaculture probably will provide some replacement employment in the medium term (to 2025). As industrial fishing and other intensified practices deplete traditional fishing grounds, many engaged in fishing cross maritime boundaries into other countries' fishing areas. These intrusions can exacerbate political tensions between neighbors with undemarcated or contested maritime or territorial boundaries.

Potential measures to ameliorate or slow the threat posed by the stresses on food security, livelihoods, and regional stability include: enhancing the scientific and technical expertise of countries in the region, expanding the capacities of institutions to better monitor the health and quantity of fish stocks and coral reef destruction, supporting regional cooperation organizations, retraining those who fish for other employment, and supporting the production of other food sources.

This page has been intentionally left blank.

Annex G

ESTIMATIVE LANGUAGE

Estimative language consists of two elements: judgments about the likelihood of developments or events occurring and levels of confidence in the sources and analytic reasoning supporting the judgments. Judgments are not intended to imply that we have proof that shows something to be a fact. Assessments are based on collected information, which is often incomplete or fragmentary, as well as logic, argumentation, and precedents.

Judgments of Likelihood. The chart below approximates how judgments of likelihood correlate with percentages. Unless otherwise stated, the Intelligence Community's judgments are not derived via statistical analysis. Phrases such as "we judge" and "we assess"—and terms such as "probable" and "likely"—convey analytical assessments.

Percent

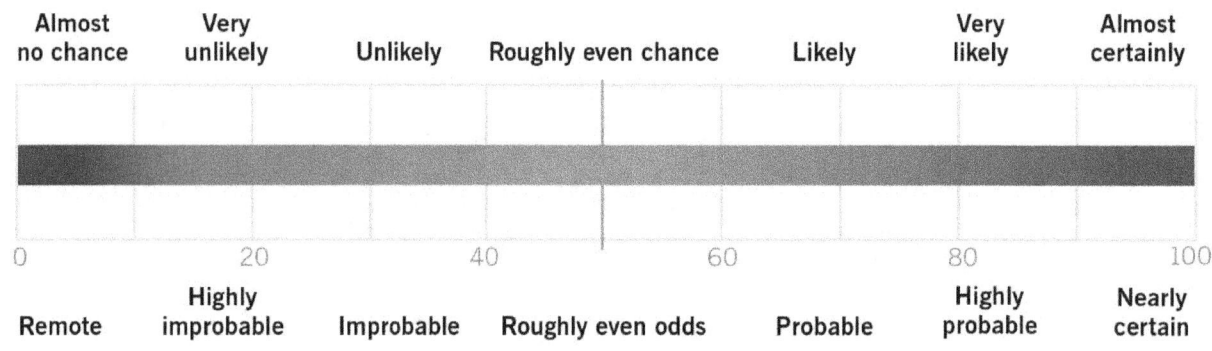

| Almost no chance | Very unlikely | Unlikely | Roughly even chance | Likely | Very likely | Almost certainly |

| 0 | 20 | 40 | 60 | 80 | 100 |

| Remote | Highly improbable | Improbable | Roughly even odds | Probable | Highly probable | Nearly certain |

Confidence in the Sources Supporting Judgments. Confidence levels provide assessments of the quality and quantity of the source information that supports judgments. Consequently, we ascribe high, moderate, or low levels of confidence to assessments:

- **High confidence** generally indicates that judgments are based on high-quality information from multiple sources. High confidence in a judgment does not imply that the assessment is a fact or a certainty; such judgments might be wrong.

- **Moderate confidence** generally means that the information is credibly sourced and plausible but not of sufficient quality or corroborated sufficiently to warrant a higher level of confidence.

- **Low confidence** generally means that the information's credibility and/or plausibility is uncertain, that the information is too fragmented or poorly corroborated to make solid analytic inferences, or that reliability of the sources is questionable.

National Intelligence Council

> The National Intelligence Council manages the Intelligence Community's estimative process, incorporating the best available expertise inside and outside the government. It reports to the Director of National Intelligence in his capacity as head of the US Intelligence Community and speaks authoritatively on substantive issues for the Community as a whole.

NIC Leadership

Chairman	Gregory Treverton
Vice Chairman	Beth Sanner
Counselor/Director, Analysis and Production Staff	Beth Sanner
Chief of Staff	Elizabeth O'Reilly
Director, Strategic Futures Group	Suzanne Fry

National Intelligence Officers

Africa	Judd Devermont
Counterintelligence	Joseph Helman
Cyber Issues	Sean Kanuck
East Asia	John Culver
Economic Issues	Rozlyn Engel
Europe	Spencer Boyer
Iran	Steven Hecker
Military Issues	J.D. Williams
The Near East	Alan Pino
North Korea	Markus Garlauskas
Russia and Eurasia	Julia Gurganus
Space & Technical Intelligence	Lawrence Gershwin
South Asia	Robert Williams
Technology	Thomas Campbell
Transnational Threats	Randall Blake
Weapons of Mass Destruction and Proliferation	Andrea Hall
Western Hemisphere	David Tapia

National Security Information

Information available as of September 2014 was used in the preparation of this product.

The following intelligence organizations participated in the <u>drafting</u> of this product:

Central Intelligence Agency (lead drafter)
Defense Intelligence Agency
National Geospatial-Intelligence Agency
National Security Agency
Department of Energy, Office of Intelligence and Counterintelligence
Department of Homeland Security, Office of Intelligence and Analysis
Department of State, Bureau of Intelligence and Research
Office of the Director of National Intelligence

The following intelligence organizations participated in the <u>coordination</u> of this product:

Central Intelligence Agency
Defense Intelligence Agency
National Geospatial-Intelligence Agency
National Security Agency
Department of Energy, Office of Intelligence and Counterintelligence
Department of Homeland Security, Office of Intelligence and Analysis
Department of State, Bureau of Intelligence and Research
Office of the Director of National Intelligence

This product was approved for publication by the National Intelligence Council.